From PLAYPENS to PROVING GROUNDS

From PLAYPENS to PROVING GROUNDS

Delbert T. Goates, M.D.
JeaNette Goates Smith

Bookcraft

SALT LAKE CITY, UTAH

Library of Congress Catalog Card Number: 87-73430
ISBN 0-88494-651-7

First Printing, 1988

Printed in the United States of America

Contents

Preface

In most cases when a celebrity and a writer collaborate as authors of a book, the celebrity has a story that will interest readers and he or she needs someone who can skillfully tell the story. Experts collaborate with writers for much the same reason. They have experience and knowledge that interests readers but they need someone to help them adequately express their discoveries.

Dr. Goates and I collaborated on this book because he possessed some important information and I had the skills to relay it to potential readers. Furthermore, having had twenty-six years of apprenticeship in the master's home, I feel doubly qualified to express Dr. Goates's child-rearing principles. As Delbert Goates's eldest child, on whom he daily practiced what he preached, I understand his ideas on two levels. I have heard him teach the concepts professionally numerous times, but I have also lived their application and experienced their effectiveness.

Despite the fact that I did the actual writing of the book, the information is presented from Dr. Goates's point of view. Such an approach seemed appropriate because the experiences related in this book are his and are best expressed in a comfortable, personal way, such as: "A patient in my office ..." or "I once knew a lad. . . ." This both alleviates the awkwardness of two "voices" and offers a warmth and character fitting to a book on rearing children. (The names used in the examples have been changed to protect the individuals' privacy.) I have used the pronouns he and she arbitrarily to reflect no gender preference.

The concepts contained in the following pages belong to Dr. Goates alone; they are derived from years of studying and practicing child-psychiatry. Nevertheless, my augmentation of the ideas makes it appropriate to attribute authorship to expert and writer alike.

I express special thanks to Claudia T. Goates, whose tremendous confidence in her family gave us the impetus to proceed with this project, and to Becky Potts, who generously volunteered professional editorial assistance.

JEANETTE GOATES SMITH

Introduction

There are too many different problems, too many different people, and too many different solutions to possibly write the "complete cookbook on child-rearing." Even a comprehensive book with detailed index that tells you how to handle each situation could never answer all your questions. Your children are unique, as are mine.

Rather than present a recipe for each possible situation, I am offering in this book principles for emotional nutrition. You may write your own recipes when you know how to cook.

This book includes much of the material I present when giving a lecture. Often after I speak, people ask me, "Where can I find a book about what you've discussed?" I know of no place where complex psychiatric principles are presented clearly, simply, and memorably enough for most parents to utilize effectively. Until now, my honest reply has therefore been, "I haven't written that book yet." But now the book is finished.

For twenty-five years I have helped children learn to govern themselves. These children seldom have major psychiatric problems such as psychoses, phobias, or manias, Neither do my patients resemble the cartoon character Ziggy, whose biggest problem is worrying about worrying about worrying. Their problems do, however, have the potential to cause major suffering in personal and interpersonal relationships. These marriages and families can suffer somewhat now—and much more later—unless change occurs.

"There are three kinds of people in this world," said Judge Payne, a New Mexico federal judge. "Those who have problems, those who have had problems, and those who are going to have problems."

No matter which category you fall into—whether you want to understand the past, troubleshoot so problems don't arise in the future, or resolve present problems you're experiencing—this book can help.

My suggestions are for normal parents who want to improve their lives and the lives of their children. This book will offer principles to help you successfully confront one of the biggest dilemmas in child-rearing today: knowing when to interfere and when to stand back.

For example, a little two-year-old boy named Danny once opened the cupboard under the kitchen sink. He spotted an unset mousetrap and started playing with it, working the spring back and forth as far as his little fingers would allow. His mother noticed the danger and said, "Danny, put that down or you will hurt your fingers. Mousetraps are dangerous." Danny kept playing with the mousetrap. Most parents would have grabbed the mousetrap to protect their son. Danny's mother let Danny decide whether he would do what she said.

What happened? *Snap!* Danny caught his fingers in the mousetrap. Mother quickly removed his fingers and comforted the sobbing child. Danny learned two important lessons: (1) mousetraps are dangerous, and (2) parents give good advice. The latter lesson is by far the more important and is best learned at age two, not as a teenager, because as Danny grows older the mousetraps will get bigger and more dangerous.

Another mother spotted her daughter playing with a mousetrap under their kitchen sink. She grabbed little Karen in time to prevent her from getting hurt.

That afternoon a baby-sitter came to stay with Karen while her mother went shopping. While the baby-sitter was watching television Karen got under the sink again to find that mousetrap. What do you think happened? *Snap!* And her mother wasn't there to comfort her or discuss the lesson she had learned.

Of course, as parents you don't want to allow your child to experiment in a way that might cause permanent damage. You would never want to teach this lesson when your child is trying to run in a busy street. In fact, I would encourage you to keep mousetraps out of a child's reach and never hurt a child deliberately while using the excuse that you were merely teaching a lesson.

The point is that you want to give your child the freedom to not always follow your advice. Warn him of the consequences. Prepare him for the potential hurt. In a situation where the pain is quick and passing, he can learn a valuable lesson about obedience.

How do you find the balance between letting a child learn to govern himself and protecting him from trouble and possible injury?

I know parents who actually leave their child alone to play in the park while they go dancing. In contrast, I know a father who grabbed a crayon out of his three-year-old's hand and said, "You don't paint horses pink." The optimal range between parental abdication and parental meddling is the basis of successful parenting.

Parenting is like a relay race. Mom and Dad carry the baton in the first lap. They make all the decisions. Later they pass the baton to their child, who has the responsibility, within his stewardship, to make decisions and complete his lap successfully.

Some parents throw the baton at their child as he prepares to run his lap. These parents abruptly drop their responsibility to make appropriate parental decisions. Other parents start to pass the baton, but they don't let go, which causes quite a tussle in the passing zone. Children develop the ability to make "best decisions" on their own when they become responsible and parents relinquish control smoothly.

From Playpens to Proving Grounds defines a happy medium between permissive and overprotective parenting. In order to help you as a parent to motivate your child to make wise decisions on his own, this book teaches four major principles:

1. The privileges you grant your children depend entirely on the degree of responsibility they demonstrate.
2. You can better motivate your children to behave when they recognize good behavior's own intrinsic rewards.
3. Allowing children to make decisions on a variety of developmental levels enables mature decision-making to occur naturally.
4. When children are in charge of their own feelings, neither self-indulgence, peers, nor parents control their happiness.

You will read a lot of stories in this book. Many are metaphorical or they teach through analogy. These will help you remember the principles because you relate to the story. The new ideas combined with the stories are intended to help you respond, "Now that makes a lot of sense to me."

Many people whom I've counseled now use metaphor in their homes. Parents use phrases when speaking to their children that you'll read in this book: "Close your castle windows," "Enjoy the hike," and "That's outside your pen." These parents do not speak the abstract and often incomprehensible language of medicine; they speak the language of metaphor. Stories, metaphors, and key phrases can help you remember successful parents' behavior when you need to. You, your spouse, even children as young as eight years of age can discuss and use these principles.

Your role as a parent today is more essential than ever before. Often when children disappoint their parents, I hear comments like, "Jim's not going to do what I say no matter what I try. I might as well let him learn the hard way until he comes around on his own."

The truth is that parents are a vital ingredient in "bringing around" a disobedient child. More than once parents have brought their child into my office and essentially said, "Fix him up, Doc. We'll be back in an hour." At such times I glance at the diplomas on my office wall to make sure I'm not a certified mechanic moving a car along an assembly line.

Your ultimate goal is to help your children do the right thing for the right reason. What child will not behave when his parents stand over him with a stick? You want your children to make *best* decisions regardless of who's watching.

Discuss the examples in this book with your child and he will learn from others' mistakes. You have heard that "experience is the best teacher." However, it's nice when that experience is someone else's, particularly if you were going to hunt mushrooms. In this book you can learn from the seasoned mushroom-hunters.

Why do I specialize in child-psychiatry? When I began to study psychiatry I noticed that many adults had painful emotional scars that, even as adults, affected their success and happiness. If helped as children, they could have overcome their problems. As adults the problems were deeply ingrained. It was this observation that convinced me to specialize in child-psychiatry so I could provide a lasting influence early in people's lives.

You have a major influence on your children, whether you perceive it or not. You can affect their lives and contribute to their eternal happiness. You can combat negative peer influences and provide them with success experiences.

Children don't want to be bad. They want to be masters of themselves. Parents should show them why it pays to govern themselves wisely and then give them the tools to do so.

1

Playpens and
Prison Bars

You probably find great joy in watching your children grow: you watch your baby lift a tiny head, roll over, then crawl, and later walk. You may call Grandma to share each new step. You don't try to prevent your toddlers from walking, because learning to walk is natural.

When you realize a new baby can roll off the bed, you put him in a crib. To prevent him from walking into the street, you put a fence around the yard. To protect him from light sockets and stairs, you may put him in a playpen.

In time your children begin to climb the trees in the backyard or ride their bikes in busy streets. Now when you call Grandma it is for advice on how to deter your children.

Grandma says wisely, "You can't put barbed wire around the bottom of every tree."

Part of a child's growth comes through "bugging" his parents. Parents may not particularly like that role, but in a sense that is the child's job.

A child's desire to try something new, to stretch his wings, to grow up, is as natural as his desire to crawl and walk. Healthy children say, "Let me try today what you wouldn't let me try yesterday."

Since part of a child's job is to "bug" his parents, a parent's job is to confront the child. By confronting the child you can make sure his desire to stretch his limits doesn't go too far. Children don't recognize their limitations as parents do. They may not recognize the dangers of tall trees and busy streets. In time they may not fear drugs, sex, or even the law, because in their independence they do not recognize their own inability.

Sometimes you will see a legitimate opportunity for your children to progress. At these times you should answer yes to their requests to try something new. At other times you must say no. When you say no and your children say yes, conflicts arise. *The nature of child-rearing involves conflict: the art of child-rearing includes reducing conflict.*

You can't avoid conflict by placing barbed wire around the bottom of every tree. Therefore, your children must learn to restrain themselves.

A Nautilus Shell

"Why did you say no?" your children will ask because they don't want to take no for an answer. Children as young as four or five may better understand your reasoning when you share the following analogy.

A snail has a shell surrounding its body. As the snail grows, so does its spiral shell. The snail cannot travel safely outside this shell and the shell protects the snail from danger.

A "shell" surrounds your child too. This is a figurative shell that I refer to as a "pen." A pen should surround each child—like a playpen that literally restrains a baby. As the child grows, the size of her "playpen" grows. Danger lurks outside the pen.

Spiral Shell

Inside the pen, a child has certain responsibilities called a "stewardship." A stewardship is simply those things for which a child is accountable. As the child matures so does the size of his stewardship.

An infant has a very small stewardship. Around six months of age her responsibility extends to her own crib; Mom won't climb in and decide which rattles she should play with. When the baby becomes a year old she plays in her bedroom as long as she doesn't climb on the dresser, jump off, and break the bed springs. When she turns two, she may play in the backyard if it's well fenced, but she can't go beyond the fence. At three years of age, she can play in the frontyard, if she stays out of the street. Around four, a child can cross a small street; at five she walks to a nearby kindergarten. This kind of progression happens naturally.

Encourage Natural Growth

"Doctor, my child isn't pushing," Mrs. Williams told me.

"In what way?"

"Melissa doesn't want to explore. She doesn't get into things like her sister did. I never have to restrain her."

It concerns me when a parent comes into my office with a child like this.

If one of your children did not bug you, if she did not push your limits, you would begin to wonder if something was wrong with her.

When a child does not "push" it may mean the child is shy. But it can also indicate a retardation. Her mental faculties, social skills, or emotional abilities may not be normal. Parents can recognize early signs of developmental delay when their child lacks the desire to explore and experience new things.

Children who do push their parents' limits are normal, healthy children. (Sometimes we just wish our children wouldn't push so hard.)

Pens That Are Too Small

Before I describe a comfortably-sized pen—the appropriate balance between a child's desire for freedom and her parents' desire for restraint—let's look at the ill effects of a pen that does not fit the child. The importance of a pen that fits is as important as the pen itself.

A pen that was too small destroyed John. John's mom and dad constantly worried about him. They always looked over his shoulder, checking to see that his ears were washed.

When John was three years old his father grabbed a crayon out of the child's hand and said, "You don't color horses pink."

Rather than prepare him for social activity, John's parents wouldn't let their son go to the school dances all his peers attended. They censored books from the school library rather than discussing their content. John was driven to school though the school was right around the corner.

One way a child can react to such overparenting is to explode. He may rebel and color horses pink just because his parents said he couldn't. Once he begins acting disobedient he will not hesitate to break his parents' important laws. Eventually, he may break greater laws and end up in a penitentiary.

John reacted in the opposite way to overparenting. His parents crushed his spirit: he became the "kid on the last row." He never raised his hand. He never got his schoolwork done. What little work he did do, he wouldn't turn in. He wouldn't even try to do things himself because he didn't think he could succeed. In his too-small pen he had no opportunity to develop confidence.

Children develop confidence when they do things by themselves, whether or not they do them "correctly." It is all right to allow your children to fail sometimes.

Once my wife came home from shopping with an interesting story. She wanted to buy my nine-year-old daughter a

Too-small Pen

dress. My wife selected two dresses in the right price range, one green dress and one blue dress. Then she asked my daughter which one she wanted.

"The green dress," she answered. My wife protested and tried to change the child's mind.

"Green looks awful on you. You have such pretty blue eyes; choose a dress to match your eyes."

"I like the green dress."

When they came home and told me what happened, I could hardly wait to look inside the sack. To my delight, I found the green dress. My little girl may not look good in green, but choosing her dress was within her stewardship. If my wife had deprived her of the choice, she would have been meddling inside my daughter's pen. (The day will come when her schoolmates will let her know whether she looks better in blue or green.)

Even small children will express adamant desires about clothing. I've seen twenty-month-old girls who would not get dressed unless they could wear their favorite shoes. As long as a child exercises her right to choose within her own stewardship, you can encourage her independent thinking.

Pens That Are Too Large

At the opposite extreme of the crushed child you will find a child in a pen that is too large. Too-large pens surrounded a lad I once treated. His parents were tired of rearing children. They had raised five children and they decided they wanted to take it easy for a while. They actually left Randy alone in the park to play while they went dancing.

You can imagine what happened to this lad with such parental abdication. Randy hopped fences and ran over the neighbor's petunia beds. When he was big enough, he hot-wired a car and took off for Las Vegas. He was picked up and sent to a place where his pen was very small . . . and the fence was quite tall.

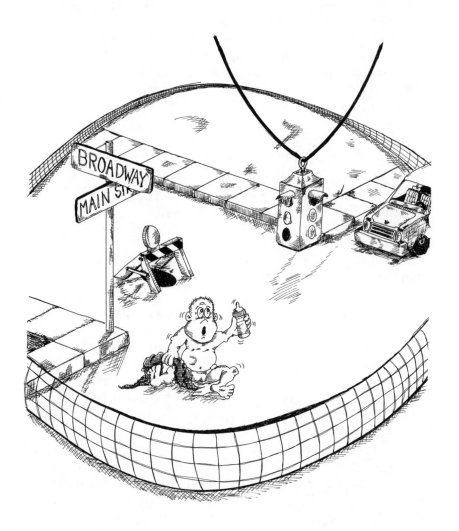

Too-large Pen

Deep inside themselves children want you to help them set limits. A young men's adviser recalled this incident from his youth:

"One time my parents let me go to a party with a group of guys I had wanted to impress. At midnight the party was still going on but I had to be home, so I asked Dave to drive me there. We pulled up in front of the house and the kitchen lights were still on. 'Oh, great, I'm in trouble,' I said. 'They waited up again.' 'You're lucky,' Dave said. 'I wish my parents cared enough just to ask me where I've been.' "

Dave started spending more and more time at Mike's house because he liked the concerned guidance and appropriate restraint shown by Mike's parents.

Children who live with parental abdication are starved for appropriate attention. Some seek friendship from adverse crowds, friends who seem like the only ones who care. Parental abdication contributes to the use of drugs, alcohol, promiscuity, and violence.

Lopsided Pens

Inappropriate pens come too small, too large, and lopsided. A pen that works must be nice and round. Sometimes I see pens with a "blowout." A pen with a blowout is nice and round, except for one side that extends beyond the child's realm of responsibility. When the pen gapes open on one side, the child wanders away from the appropriate behavior.

A twelve-year-old whom I'll call Bryan took his mother's car keys, drove the car down the street, and bounced it off three of the neighbor's parked cars. The police recognized this as unnaturally bad behavior for a boy with no other major behavior problems, so they sent Bryan to my office, rather than to the juvenile detention home. After visiting with Bryan, I found that his problem was not stealing cars. His problem was that he wanted a bicycle. He did not own a

Lopsided Pen

bicycle and there was no real good reason for him not to own a bicycle. In fact, Bryan even earned sufficient money to buy one.

After visiting with Bryan's mother, I learned that she had lost a brother who was hit by a car while riding a bicycle. Therefore, she was very nervous about bicycles. That was the mother's problem. Bryan didn't even dare confront her about a bicycle because at one level he recognized that as an intolerable discussion topic. Stealing the car was Bryan's attempt to enlarge his pen on one side when his mother was pushing in on the other side. When Bryan's father found out that his son needed a bicycle, he bought the boy a bicycle. Once the blowout in Bryan's pen was mended, he started behaving normally. (However, the mother came unglued, so for six months I helped her get over the death of her brother, which she had never really resolved.)

Either parent may have a hang-up in a particular situation. One advantage of two parents is that they can discuss personal hang-ups and work together on rounding out the pen.

Parents create lopsided pens when they allow children some precocious privileges and deny them other more common privileges. When parents allow a ten-year-old daughter to dress in designer brand miniskirts and heavy makeup, she feels like a teenager. However, they do not let her date or go to the dances the teenagers attend, so her pen fits in some places but in others is too big. Parents must decide that the ten-year-old is not old enough for teenage privileges and stop tempting her by pretending she is a teenager.

Sometimes children develop more rapidly in some areas than others, which tempts parents to give them a larger pen. How do you treat a child who does so well in school that she is asked to skip a grade? Intellectually she is as responsible as a fifth grader; however, emotionally she is still as responsible as a fourth grader. Children asked to skip a grade face a difficult situation.

There are parents who will not allow their children, however bright, to skip a grade because of the social hazards involved. Other parents find they must carefully monitor their child and help the child understand that even though she is in the fifth grade, her pen is still the fourth-grade size that she can handle, until she earns a larger pen.

Pens with Gaps

Two parents sometimes provide a disadvantage in establishing the size of the child's pen. If parents do not agree on the size of the pen, the child will choose whichever size he likes. When Mother wants the pen to be one size and Dad wants it another, the child's pen will look like two giant C's that face each other but do not touch.

You won't keep very many sheep in a pen with huge gaps. You might as well not even mention pens to a child if he doesn't know what his pen looks like.

Even more important than the exact size of the pen is that parents act together and support one another. Come to an agreement on the size of each child's pen.

Parents Who Get Together

To reduce conflict, parents can discuss the size of their child's pen with one another. Mom and Dad need to determine together what size of pen each child can handle. One of the great advantages of two parents is that they can sit down and have a meeting where they both can help decide the size of the pen.

The parents can discuss the various issues and decide together when and how much to increase the size of the pen. The child, in a sense, is "outnumbered."

In a one-parent family, it's "one against one" and that turns into a battle of wills.

Pen with Gaps

The child says, "I want . . ."

The parent says, "No, you can't . . ."

"Why not?"

"Because I said so."

When you get into a battle of wills with a teenager, it helps to have the clout of two opinions. If you're a single parent, discussing the size of the child's pen with someone else may help you arrive at an optimal size. Grandma may care as much as a spouse, and perhaps she could discuss the child's pen with you. Or maybe you have a close friend of the family who knows the children well. In either case you can say, "Grandma and I have carefully thought it over and we decided . . ." Not only is the child outranked but also outnumbered. In addition, Grandma or your friend may recognize your particular hang-ups.

If you do not know the size of the child's pen, your child will learn to manipulate you. If one parent gives a child permission to go duck hunting and one doesn't, a child will learn quickly which parent to ask for permission to hunt ducks.

A young man named Phil told me how he wanted to learn to shoot a BB gun. His dad didn't know whether that activity fit in Phil's pen or not. Dad told Phil to ask his mother. Mom said, "I don't care, ask your father." Phil told his father, "Mom said it was okay." Phil can become a law unto himself when his parents don't agree upon the size of his pen.

Children manipulate a parent who is strict in one area and liberal in another. Phil knows Dad will let him go play ball when Mom makes him stay home and clean a messy room. But Mom will let him go to the church activity night when Dad makes him stay home and mow the lawn. In either case, Phil knows who to ask to get his own way.

Somewhere in between these cases of too much parenting, parental abdication, and lopsided rules is a nice, comfortable pen. Parents who give their child a nice, comfortable pen care for their child without crushing him. A comfortable pen gives the child room enough to do his own thing while maintaining the security of parents who take care of him so that he doesn't run in front of a Mack truck. The next chapter shows you how to determine what size pen is comfortable for each child.

2

How to Determine the Size of the Pen

$\mathbf{A}$ six-foot-tall freshman in high school came into my office one day. His brother had just been arrested for auto theft. "Mom and Dad are going to be so strict with me now," Peter said. "After what my brother's done, they won't let me drive until I'm twenty."

"Not if you prove yourself more responsible than your brother," I said. "If you are smart and you keep your act together, how can they deny you the privileges you ask?" The theory behind determining the size of a child's pen is: Responsibility earns privileges.

Peter understood the fairness of this rule. He determined to earn his privileges. The logic of this rule seldom leaves children room to argue. Teenagers especially appreciate this approach because they are concerned with fairness.

To help your children accept this idea, explain that the privileges they receive relate directly to how much responsibility they demonstrate within their stewardship. Also, teach them what responsibility means.

Discuss the Pen with the Child

The analogies in this chapter are suitable to share with your children. They can enable your youngsters to understand that everyone must tolerate limits. This understanding helps reduce conflict that occurs when you want a pen to be one size and your child wants a bigger one.

Pens even surround adults. I can't do everything I want. I own keys to my office suite, but not to every office in the building. I knock before I go into my neighbor's house. Adults respect the space of other people.

Sometimes literal limits surround people. In New England they say, "Good fences make good neighbors." Neighbors mow their own lawns and keep the stereo volume low, but they do not go next door and tell Mr. Jones what vegetables to plant in his garden or which music to play. Neighbors act responsibly on their side of the fence but do not dictate the care of someone else's backyard. The idea of fences applies not only to neighbors but also to family relationships. Children, like adults, learn to prove accountable for their own lives and to tolerate the limits placed upon them.

You may leave snacks in the cookie jar for the children to eat, but the children cannot claim free access to every drawer in your bedroom. Your daughter may play with the dolls in her room, but she cannot go into her older sister's room and listen to her sister's records without asking permission.

A Parental Role

Adolescents particularly need to understand the necessity of pens. One day I asked fourteen-year-old Ryan this question: "If you were standing in your front yard and saw the little three-year-old neighbor boy dash out into the street, what would you do?"

"Why, I'd stop him," Ryan said.

"He's not your brother," I said. "You could raise your eyebrows and say, 'That truck will probably miss him.' "

"But somebody needs to protect the kid from getting hurt," Ryan said.

I compared Ryan's desire to save his neighbor to his parents' role in protecting him from danger.

Ryan saw that in restraining his neighbor, he would act in a parental role. Likewise, when a thirteen-year-old wants to drive without a license, someone must restrain him. Adolescents begin to see that you can no more neglect your responsibility to set limits than they could allow a three-year-old to run in front of a truck.

Part of being a parent is looking into a mirror and feeling comfortable that you set appropriate limits. If you decided not to set limits and allowed your child to run loose, that would not give you parental satisfaction.

When an adolescent begins to recognize your need to feel comfortable with your judgment, he becomes more willing to accept the parental role. He knows what it means to take on that role himself with regard to other younger children.

Adolescents also realize that when they get outside of an appropriate pen Mom and Dad become anxious. When parents get anxious their teens will likely get even less freedom.

Though parents need to respond to irresponsible behavior with less freedom, I am concerned when I see parents who tighten a child's pen too much, too frequently, or for too long. If parents get inside a child's crib and begin to pick his rattles for him, how will the child feel? Adolescents in particular recognize meddling and unfair restraints. As you discuss pens with your children you will find an optimal compromise between appropriate parental restraint and the child's desire for freedom.

You may be familiar with "kid contracts." With contracts the parents make the child's decisions and the child agrees to abide by them, so the contracts enforce the rules, rather than the parents. This, however, leaves the parents in control.

A major difference exists between pens and contracts. The size of a child's pen is determined by how well he handles responsibility. He decides how much responsibility he can handle. The object of establishing limits or pens is to put the child in control. Let him demonstrate his ability to perform in any given sized pen. If a child demonstrates his ability to handle a particular sized pen, Mom and Dad have no right to make decisions inside that pen.

Age Is Not a Criteria

It would be nice if you could look up the formula for "fair restraints" in the manual you got when you brought your child home from the hospital. But the nurses do not hand out a bible on child-rearing along with the Pampers. There is no such thing as a manual that says, "When a child is ten years old he gets forty-one privileges." You cannot follow a formula for rearing children the way you follow a formula to figure insurance tables. You must determine the correct size of each child's pen individually.

If you observe several children of the same age, you will realize that age alone cannot provide the criteria to determine the size of a child's pen. Mary reads at a second-grade level like a seven-year-old, and Brad reads at a ninth-grade level like a fourteen-year-old. Yet, both Mary and Brad are ten-year-olds who attend the same fifth-grade class. Their reading age level varies 100 percent.

The maturity level of two children the same age can vary 100 percent as well. Age does not determine a child's accountability.

A family visited my office once and I saw a remarkable example of how age does not determine accountability. I asked the mother what she saw as the problem. "Frank [her six-year-old] is raising holy pandemonium," she said. "I can't understand why he misbehaves so badly."

I asked her about the other children in the family. "We also have an eight-year-old son, Scott," she said. "But he is retarded." As we talked, I learned that this mother would not give six-year-old Frank privileges that she denied eight-year-old retarded Scott. She thought it unfair that a six-year-old be allowed privileges that an eight-year-old couldn't handle, and she set limits by age. This caused Frank to explode because he was deprived of freedoms he could easily handle.

The size of the pen has little to do with whether the child is six or eight. It has nothing to do with whether "everybody else in the neighborhood is doing it" or if "older brother and sister got to do it when they were my age." A child must learn how to earn privileges.

How to Get a Larger Pen

Since responsibility earns privileges, a child can earn a larger pen by fulfilling his responsibilities. A child may wonder what his responsibilities include, and they will vary with each child.

One child may be required to make his bed, pick up his clothes, and leave the bathroom clean. Another child may be held accountable for maintaining a *B* average in school, taking care of the baby when Mother goes shopping, or looking at the chore list and finishing her chores without being asked.

When your child can accomplish all you require of her and she asks, "Mother, will you increase my privileges?" you will find it very hard to tell her no. She obviously demonstrates considerable responsibility inside her pen. She knows how to earn privileges.

I knew a young man of fourteen who behaved so responsibly he was treated like a guest in his own home. His mother did not tell him when to come and go or how to spend his time.

The young man provides more of a resource to his mother than his mother provides to him. He learned the system. He learned that if he was very, very responsible, he could do almost anything he asked to do. And if he did everything responsibly, why shouldn't he?

I asked this boy one day, "Bruce, what sort of work are you going to do to make money this year?"

He said, "Well, I don't have a job, but I think I've got something better." My ears perked up.

"What's better than a job to earn money?"

"Well, I've got a deal where I'm going to make about three bucks an hour working for a couple of hours a day on my own time, wearing my own clothes, and staying indoors."

That sounded awfully good because he could even pick his hours. This was his plan: he figured that if he got straight A's he could get a college scholarship for board, room, and tuition. He amortized this over four years of high school at two hours a day, and that equaled over three dollars an hour. At fourteen, he could not get a better job.

This boy thought ahead. As a result he not only received a full scholarship for his undergraduate work but when he finished college he also received a four-year scholarship to Harvard to do graduate work in political science. He got paid all the way through school because he learned the system: Responsibility earns privileges.

Children Who Learn the System

If a child does not know the appropriate way to earn more privileges, she needs to learn. You must help your child recognize that the way she can get a bigger pen is similar to the way she got from third grade to fourth grade. If she works hard in the third grade she goes to fourth grade. If she works hard in the fourth grade she goes to fifth grade. If she works hard in the fifth grade she goes to sixth grade. If she doesn't work the teachers may hold her back in the same grade, and if she really fails they will send her back to repeat the previous grade.

Learning responsibility teaches children a very important lesson. Most systems work just like our schools do in advancing students from grade to grade. Those who act responsibly and do a good job increase their opportunities for promotion.

Ask a child, "How do you get a larger pen at your house?" Frequently the child will say, "I don't know," or he will say, "I just pester, and pester, and pester until my parents finally give in." A bright little boy in my office actually said, "If I beg long enough I know my parents will eventually give in." When a child learns that if he pesters long enough his parents will reward him by giving in, the child becomes a little pest.

Don't Buck the System

Parents must be careful not to create inappropriate exceptions to the rule, "responsibility earns privileges." If you allow children privileges that they do not earn, they are falsely rewarded and do not learn the system.

Joyce told her daughter Sue, "You can go downtown with your friends after your room is clean."

When Sue's friends came over, her room still had clothes spread all over an unmade bed. She begged her mom, "Please, my friends are already here. I don't want to make them wait. I promise, I'll clean my room when I get home." Joyce let Sue go.

That evening when Sue came home she said, "Oh please, Mom, this is the best show, it won't ever be on TV again." Sue didn't clean her room. Children catch on fast when parents don't mean what they say.

Other children think that if they ask enough times their parents will get sick of the question and say, "Oh, all right, go ahead."

Ten-year-old Robby wanted to shoot his BB gun before Dad came home from work. "Wait for your father," Mother said, "or I'll take the gun away for good." Robby didn't wait and shot the gun anyway. When Mother took the gun, Robby resorted to sweet talk and promises.

"Please, please, Mom," he said. "I'll listen to you next time; I'll be careful." Mother wanted to give in because she was tired of Robby's persistence, but she kept her promise— and the gun.

One of the main reasons parents give in to a persistent child is because they lack the energy to follow through. Sue had more energy to withstand her mother's requests to clean the room than her mother had to keep checking the room and asking if it was clean. Tireless children will break the rules again and again. Or they will beg until their parents break down. An alert mom or dad can withstand a smart, persistent child.

It will be less difficult to hold your ground when your request is reasonable. The mother who says, "If you watch that violent movie while I'm gone, I'll throw out the television," is only making a threat. When it comes time to throw out the television few mothers could do it. (Although I know some who have.) Children recognize idle threats and soon learn to disregard them. Instead, a mother who says, "If you watch that violent movie, I will have the cable station disconnected," is more likely to follow through on her promise.

Both you and your children should know the system for getting a larger pen. Your children will know you are serious when you give them direction and you won't change the system. When your children know you don't give in to pests, they are less likely to pester you.

3

A Key
Relationship

There are many different ways to tighten a child's pen when he's been irresponsible and as many ways to enlarge a pen when he behaves. Regardless of which method you choose, it will work best when you have a good relationship with your child.

Have you ever wondered why a child behaves for one parent and not for the other? Why does your child respond so well to his teacher one year and the next year he has problems? The answer often lies in the relationship the teacher, or the parent, establishes with the child. The effective teacher develops a firm, fair, and friendly relationship with her class before teaching. The effective parent develops a loving, resourceful relationship with his children before disciplining.

A ten-year-old girl told me an interesting story. Throughout her fifth-grade year she found herself repeatedly in the principal's office. She didn't get along with her teacher, and at the slightest provocation the teacher sent her to the principal.

By the time February came the little girl knew the principal quite well. She sent him a valentine that said "To my friend the principle." The next day the principal called her into his office. She knew she hadn't done anything wrong so she was glad for the chance to visit. As she walked in the principal's office he put his arm around her shoulder and gave her a big hug. "Thanks for the valentine," he said. "I want to show you something." He pulled out the card and pointed to the misspelled "principle." "When you're writing to me, I want you to remember I'm your 'pal.' You can address the card to the 'principal' [he wrote the correctly spelled word]: 'P-R-I-N-C-I-P-A-L,' because I'm your pal and also your friend." She smiled at her newly found friend. Her behavior problem soon decreased and then disappeared because she had a "pal" who wanted her to succeed in fifth grade.

This little girl changed her behavior because she found someone who cared for her. Three-fourths of the reason a child responds to a consequence is because of his relationship with the person who gives him the consequence. One-fourth of the response is determined by the consequence itself. In some relationships you can merely mention a mistake and the child will change. The child respects you and wants the reward of your admiration.

If you would like your child to change his behavior there are a number of steps he must follow, as explained below.

Steps to Change

When a person in therapy seeks guidance he follows five steps to change: insight, guilt, compensation, commitment, and improvement. To help patients remember these same five steps, I teach them what is sometimes called "the five R's of repentance."

Repentance Comparison

Change	Repentance	Action
1. Insight	Recognition	See the mistake
2. Guilt	Remorse	Feel sorry
3. Compensation	Restitution	Pay back the injured person
4. Commitment	Resolve	Promise not to do that again
5. Improvement	Reform	Follow through on promise

When a child makes a mistake, he cannot change until he follows these steps. He first must recognize he behaved badly (1). For instance, if Tommy stole Katie's Twinkie out of her lunch, he needs to feel sorry (2). He then gives her a Twinkie to replace the one he stole (3). Next he promises not to steal her Twinkies anymore (4). Finally Tommy makes right his wrong by never again stealing from lunches (5).

Confrontation

Many people understand these five necessary steps. However, there is a step preceding recognition that few people welcome. I call this step "confrontation." Often I confront a patient with behavior that he or she may not know causes problems. Many people cannot even recognize the behavior or attitude that causes the problem unless someone confronts them and explains it properly.

If a patient can come into my office and describe the behavior or attitude that led to their problem, they are well on their way to solving it. Confrontation is hard to achieve alone because people are naturally defensive. With my patients, I am the first one to help them decide where to begin the process of change. I lead them to the mirror, polish it, and say, "This is how I, and possibly others, perceive you." (You see, when you look in the mirror the left ear is always on the right side. People do not see their faces as they appear to others.)

Children, as much as adults, need someone to confront them. Your daughter may not even realize that drinking milk directly from the cereal bowl is impolite.

Confrontation is a vital step in helping people change: I see it happen in my office daily. I therefore see value in augmenting this list and putting this additional step first, before the five steps of change or repentance. But I can't teach the five R's of repentance and then throw in a step that starts with a C.

In both ancient and modern times the Lord has in essence said, "Those whom I love, I will chastize, and I will *reprove* and *rebuke* them" (see Hebrews 12:6, D&C 95:1 – 2). *Reproof.* That is a good R word that means the same thing as confront in this context. But notice that the Lord speaks of more than just reproof and rebuke. We are to not only reprove those whom we love but also love them more after doing so (see D&C 121:43).

At first your children will probably not believe you when you tell them you reprove them because you love them. Actually, if children realized how much you could help them, they might actually ask you to reprove them. However, I have yet to meet a child who had to ask to be reproved. Children know that "even if your own best friend won't tell you, your mother will."

Reproof

Children will come to believe that you reprove them because you love them only if you reprove with love. Two restraints on reproof will assure that the reproof is done with love: (1) Reprove only when necessary and (2) reprove only for the benefit of the recipient.

When parents constantly reprove, children cease to listen. Like the boy who cried "wolf," some parents cry, "Don't do that! Stay away from there! Naughty, naughty!" all day long. When parents need to reprove for a very important reason (i.e., the pan on the stove is hot and could seriously hurt them), children who have heard "wolf, wolf" too often will not regard important warnings. Infrequent reproof will occur naturally if the child understands his responsibilities, as discussed in chapter 2. Though you reprove only when necessary, you may have to say it twice or raise your voice if your child will not listen.

Reproof for the benefit of the recipient is different from "getting it off your chest." If you've got to get something off your chest, punch a punching bag or write in your journal. Then come in and talk to the little one who made a mistake. (Chapter 4 shows how consequences must benefit the recipient.)

The ultimate way to reprove with love is to reprove and afterwards show forth an increase in love (see D&C 121:43). That means after you speak loudly to get Janie's attention or to send Janie to her room, go in and sit on Janie's bed. Put your arm around her, tell her you love her and *teach* as you reprove. (See chapter 5.)

Start with Love

If you will show an "increase in love" after you reprove, you must have some love in the first place. Few children respond to reproof from someone they don't know. They will not even respond when you reprove unless a relationship exists between the two of you.

You will need to have some love for and some type of relationship with the child who made the mistake before you will have any influence on him. For example, if you were driving on the main drag in town and some teenager cut his car in front of you, how much influence do you think you would have if you stuck your head out of the window to yell at him. The teenager would probably be even more discourteous. You do not have a relationship with the teenager and therefore have no influence over him at all.

When somebody goes in to see the minister, he says, "You're the minister, I'm the parishioner. Help me straighten this out." When somebody comes into my office, they say, "Doctor, I've got a problem. You're the doctor. I'm the patient. Tell me how I ought to handle it." In one case a doctor-patient relationship exists. In the other, the relationship is between the minister and his parishioner. Even if this relationship is not emotionally close, the structure of the relationship allows growth to occur.

Jeopardizing the Relationship

Sometimes in families parents have so jeopardized their relationship with the children—so strained their love—that they do not exert the influence that they want.

Of all of the relationships you maintain, a positive relationship with your family is the most important. With them you will want to have the most influence. Maintaining that relationship is more important than the exact consequences that you give your children. You will not want to jeopardize that relationship with excessive consequences or with a self-concern that is greater than your child-concern.

How can you avoid jeopardizing the relationship? Sometimes you must discuss the problem with the child before you give a consequence, to find out how he feels. If he adamantly feels that consequences are inappropriate, you would actually jeopardize the relationship by imposing those consequences. When he is ready for a consequence, it will be effective. If a child has no recognition and no remorse, taking restitution from him prematurely won't do any good. As far as he's concerned, you just robbed him. The key is to go through the process of change step by step: step one, reprove the child; step two, bring about recognition of the error.

The relationship of a coach with the players on his ball team illustrates one way to avoid jeopardizing a relationship.

I watched this scene at a Little League baseball game. In the bottom of the last inning the bases were loaded, the score tied, with two outs and a full count.

The little pitcher stood trembling on the pitcher's mound. He knew his next pitch could lose the ball game or keep his team's hopes alive. And if his team went on to win the game they would win the championship.

Right before the pitcher threw the ball the coach walked out onto the pitcher's mound. That coach put his arm around the little boy and gave him a speech. I couldn't hear what he said.

He may have said, "You knucklehead, you blockhead. We almost had the game won and look at the mess you've gotten us into. Do you realize what this game means? So help me, boy, if you don't throw a perfect ball this time, you'll never pitch for me again."

Or he may have said, "Relax, Joey. This is just a game. Cool down and throw the ball. Give it your best shot. I want you to know that whatever happens you'll be back on the mound pitching the next game. You're my man. I have confidence in you."

That child stopped trembling and threw a curve ball that would make some major league pitchers jealous. The batter swung with all his might as the ball passed by him and landed in the catcher's mitt. I knew right away what that coach had whispered to my son on the mound.

Which type of coach are you?

No Time for a Relationship

Often people will witness the misbehavior of a child they don't know. If my ten-year-old son picked up a matchbox car in K Mart and put it in his pocket, I would want someone to do something about it. If an individual witnessed the theft and did nothing about it, that person would in a sense be aiding and abetting the crime. The witness could choose to confront the child, even though he had a less effective relationship with the child, or the person could contact someone more effective. The store owner has a type of a relationship already established as the owner of the stolen merchandise; nevertheless, the parents would want to help the boy recognize his mistake and prepare him to receive an appropriate consequence.

In parts of the Polynesian islands, parents rear children collectively and even pass them around. In our society, I have seen people carefully attend to their own children and totally neglect a misbehaving child right at their feet.

An adult may not have a relationship enabling him to provide the most effective consequence, but for the child's benefit he should point out the misbehavior to whoever has a relationship with the child.

I could not offer therapy to help people change unless the first step, reproof, began the improvement process. But this new step can backfire. If you reprove with love, or without a meaningful relationship, you will not achieve anything. Once you have established a relationship it is time to consider which of the numerous consequences might encourage appropriate behavior.

4

Expanding the Pitchfork Theory

Tommy ran to his room and slammed the door. "You can't take my firecrackers," he yelled. "I bought them with my own money." His mother screamed back, "You're grounded," but Tommy did not respond. He was already making plans to buy more firecrackers—and he knew just where he could hide them next time.

Which of the many consequences for behavior will encourage children to do what's right? You may have found a consequence that worked one time with one child yet it elicited a 180-degree different response the next time. What hope is there in parenting then? What happened to the rule book on child-rearing?

The popular theories suppose that when a child does something good you pat him on the back; for a bad deed you aim a little lower. You could illustrate this theory with a diagram that looks like a pitchfork. On the right side there are negative consequences, and on the left side there are positive consequences.

Pitchfork Theory

No wonder parents get discouraged with child-rearing. This approach just doesn't always work. Positive and negative consequences are too black and white and don't illustrate all optimal consequences.

It is very difficult to predict a child's behavior. If you give a rat a consequence, he reacts predictably. Scientists observe rats again and again to formulate their theories and the rats behave consistently. Children, however, don't always react as their parents expect them to.

The popular theory of positive and negative consequences may work in a laboratory: it can make dogs drool and rats run mazes. But people are not dogs or rats!

The person who wants to become a dog trainer studies for about ninety days. It doesn't take long to learn to train dogs. The person who wants to become a child-psychiatrist, for instance, must study for thirteen years after high school. Even then he will continue to learn new things about children throughout his lifetime. People are far more complex than dogs.

A Consequence Continuum

Because children are so complex, parents must experiment with a variety of consequences. A more accurate picture of consequences for behavior would look like a straight line rather than a pitchfork. There are many, many stops along the continuum.

Some of the consequences on the continuum are not imposed by parents or other authority figures. They "just happen." I have labeled these nonimposed consequences on the left end of the continuum as "natural consequences," and on the right end of the continuum as "fulfilled ego." As a child matures he needs less and less parental direction. He is more inclined to be motivated by natural consequences and a fulfilled ego.

Consequences Continuum

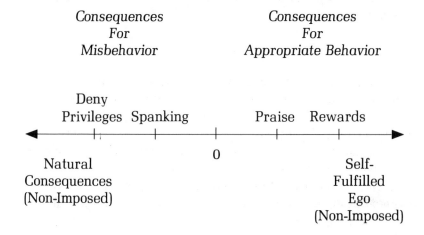

Consequences
For
Misbehavior

Consequences
For
Appropriate Behavior

Deny
Privileges Spanking

Praise Rewards

0

Natural
Consequences
(Non-Imposed)

Self-
Fulfilled
Ego
(Non-Imposed)

The nonimposed consequences for misbehavior are usually unpleasant. The natural consequence of playing with fire may be a burnt finger. Neither Mom nor Dad caused that to happen, but the lesson is profound.

The nonimposed consequence for appropriate behavior, such as earning good grades in school, is more effective than consequences Mom, Dad, or teachers impose. Children who behave well discover a "fulfilled ego" provides satisfaction beyond consequences that are imposed.

The consequences closest to "zero" on the continuum are the least effective in changing behavior. Those at either end are the most effective, as they are less parent-imposed and have a greater long-term effect. Nonimposed consequences motivate children and adolescents to do what's right when no one is around to tell them how to behave.

For the next three chapters I will discuss some of the consequences along the continuum. These consequences can indeed change behavior as long as they are not abused or misused. The consequences for children who behave include praise, rewards, and a fulfilled ego; and those for misbehavior include chastisement, loss of privileges, and natural consequences.

Praise

Dogs respond as predictably to praise as they do to dog biscuits. They don't second guess their master's motives. However, a child's intellect causes him to react to praise in a number of different ways.

Praise may motivate some children to repeat good behavior, while others are not affected by it. Praise that is well-deserved and offered in a sincere manner works most of the time. But unless parents heed certain cautions, their children may be turned off by praise.

Sincerity Counts

A grown woman visited my office who recognized she was lacking self-esteem. She didn't have the confidence to accept callings or assignments, however simple.

As we visited, we discovered childhood praise had destroyed Mrs. Johnson's self-esteem. She found this difficult to accept because her parents had praised her all the time. She could still remember the types of things they praised her for.

Her parents complimented her on tasks that she considered menial, like matching her bows to her dresses or keeping her dolls off the floor. They praised her *B* grades when she knew she could have earned *A*'s.

They complimented her so much that the words became meaningless. "Dad would tell me I looked lovely without even looking up from his newspaper," Mrs. Johnson recalled.

Because Mrs. Johnson felt no satisfaction in the accomplishments her parents praised her for, the praise itself provided no satisfaction. She felt inadequate because she wanted to accomplish something really noteworthy, and she never felt able because her parents were so satisfied with what she considered mediocrity.

Small children respond most readily to praise because they are less able to second guess their parents' motives. Yet even toddlers can detect a parent who praises only because he wants to control the child's behavior.

When my grandchildren came to visit me one Christmas, their mother was eager to show me all the things they had learned that year. She told the boys how proud she was that they were so bright and encouraged them to perform for Grandpa.

"You are such big boys, sing 'I Am a Child of God' for Grandpa." The boys squirmed and hid their faces in their mother's lap. "Okay, tell Grandpa what Practical Pig says." My grandsons whispered a few words and then said, "I don't want to."

"That was a very good start. I know you can say the whole thing." Their mother encouraged them to finish their recitation without success.

Even these two- and three-year-olds could tell they were being manipulated. Though their mother sincerely admired her toddlers' ability to perform, it would have been hard to convince them that her praise was sincere and not intended to manipulate.

Praise That Is Too Intense

At an assembly, the principal of a local school invited the most outstanding student in the sixth grade onto the stage. He placed his arm around Ralph and told the whole school about him. Ralph earned a 4.0 that year. He won the track and field blue ribbon. He was an Eagle Scout. The principal continued to compliment and praise this student.

After the assembly Ralph wished the scene had never happened. He felt embarrassed because he did not have the capacity to deal with such an abundance of praise.

When children turn eight or nine they start to take responsibility for their own actions, and praise becomes more meaningful. They realize the praise they receive is entirely dependent on their performance.

Being emotionally inexperienced, youth have difficulty dealing with an overabundance of positive feelings; their tummies can only hold so much pie. As children grow older they learn to accept praise graciously and their capacity to tolerate praise increases.

However, before they reach the point where they can accept praise graciously, even a small amount of praise, particularly when offered in front of a child's peers, can be too intense.

A little girl named Mary once experienced this type of praise. I counseled with Mary's mother, who complained because her once-exemplary daughter suddenly became rebellious. Mary had been an ideal child. Her big blue eyes and blonde curls caused adults and children both to pay excessive attention to her. Mary's mother loved to tell everybody about her daughter's prestigious roles in community ballet theater. She dressed Mary in expensive clothes; Mary earned excellent grades and repeatedly won piano competitions. She always volunteered to help at school and at home. Her good behavior seemed to come naturally.

The change came when Mary's siblings and friends started teasing her: "You're a goody two shoes." "Mary's teacher's pet." In order to gain acceptance from her peers, Mary stopped being the ideal child. She did things that she knew would cause her mother to yell at her so that her friends or siblings could hear. Acceptance by her peers and siblings concerned Mary far more than the praise of adults.

Around age six or seven, when children start school, they become acutely aware of what other people think about them. Most often the opinion of their peers means more to them than the opinion of their parents. And at seven it's not "cool" to do everything Mother says.

Becoming Bereft of Praise

Adults who as children received praise that was either insincere or too intense make it a habit to dismiss all praise. Even individuals who were praised sincerely as children might avoid compliments because they learned from others that to accept praise is inappropriate. When given a compliment, "You did a good job. You played that piece beautifully," the individual will often respond, "Aw, not really."

Learning to graciously accept and enjoy gifts and compliments is a motivational experience. Embarrassed denial, nervous self-criticism, or a "get even" I'll-return-the-favor attitude destroys the praise and the joy in giving praise.

The danger of false modesty is that children follow this example and become bereft of praise. Sincere, valid praise is essential to an individual's self-esteem. Many adults who complain of depression will *not allow* others to uplift them; they turn compliments around.

My daughter had a refreshing experience with a little Greek girl who had not been taught false modesty. "I heard you're a pretty good baby-sitter," my daughter said to her thirteen-year-old neighbor. "Yes, I'm very good," she replied sweetly. All children, like the Greek girl, should be allowed to accept appropriate praise without fear of immodesty.

When praise is offered in a sincere manner, without intent to manipulate or embarrass, it may at times motivate some children to improve their behavior. However, the real benefit of praise is in building a child's self-esteem.

In order to choose a consequence to motivate your child, listen to your child. Discover what's going on in his mind. How is he responding to praise? Then select a consequence accordingly.

5

What's in It
for Me?

What encourages some mothers to wash and iron and clean house? The mother could do it because the father pays the mortgage, but the father would probably pay the mortgage even if the mother did not get the wash done. So why does the mother do it?

The mother knows that if she invites guests to dinner and popcorn is scattered all over the front room rug, somebody must clean up that rug. The front room rug is a part of the mother's ego. A messy rug reflects on her self-esteem. The mother would no more leave a mess of popcorn on the front room floor with special guests coming than you would go to church without washing your face. The mother's ego includes whether she is taking good care of her stewardship, which includes the front room rug. A satisfied ego is part of the mother's reward for her household duties.

Those who think a toddler's ego includes the front room rug kid themselves. He doesn't care if there are spots on the front room rug. Sometimes parents forget that two-year-olds cannot comprehend abstract ego rewards such as pride in a clean house. Toddlers need more immediate, concrete rewards for keeping the popcorn out of the living room. Rewards, the step after praise on the consequences continuum (see chapter 4), may provide another successful way to motivate good behavior.

Rewards

Suppose you just got promoted to vice-president of sales and marketing for a company. The president of the company comes to you and says, "We need an increase in cash flow or we will fold. If we don't increase sales next month we will be out of business, and so will the little old ladies who sew bibs in the back room. You must get going."

Tomorrow you will meet with your ten salesmen. What will you tell them to make sure you achieve your goals? Will you tell them the same thing the president told you? If you tell them that they will lose their jobs unless they get on the stick, they may go look for new jobs tomorrow (or go home and go to bed for a week).

One of the reasons some companies hire a vice-president in charge of sales and marketing is to protect the salesmen from presidents who may be more concerned about cash flow and interest rates than employee turnover. Salesmen are probably not concerned about the company's cash flow and interest rates. Salesmen need something else to make sure they achieve their goals. They need to know, "What's in it for me?"

The first salesman that gets 150 percent of his usual quota might win a trip to Hawaii. The next three salesmen might receive a trip to Las Vegas. They want to receive some type of a reward or motivation. A negative incentive will only burden them. Rewards, incentives, motivation, and bonuses start salesmen moving.

If you struggle to get your children to reach goals, you will recognize the brilliance in rewards. You do not have to bribe your kids. A bribe is illegal money for an illegal activity. A reward is a perfectly honest incentive for a job well done.

Cautions

Some people might say that if you offer your child a reward every time you want something of her she will resent you for controlling her. This is hogwash. Much of life is based on rewards. Your boss will usually reward you for good performance by giving you a raise. The university will reward you for good grades by offering you a scholarship. Your wife might reward you for cleaning out the garage with a big kiss. God rewards you for keeping his commandments by letting you into heaven.

Rewards do not need to be material. You do not have to bring home a surprise every time you leave your child with a baby-sitter. This teaches your child, "I'd better threaten misbehavior or Mom will forget my surprise." Rewards for mature behavior can come in the form of privileges (a larger pen) as well as gifts. Your children will learn that privileges, such as a later bedtime, are to be earned, as discussed in chapter 1.

When your children become adolescents, "what's in it for them" might be that their ego feels good, like when Mom vacuums the front room. "What's in it for them" might be that they helped the community they belong to by not littering. "What's in it for them" might be that they get to go to heaven.

You will be happy to know you don't have to wear yourself out trying to reward every good deed. "Fulfilled ego" at the end of the consequences continuum represents the self-motivated, self-fulfilled adolescent who finds his own reward. No one imposes the consequences: adolescents learn themselves the value of each good decision. .

No adolescent becomes self-fulfilled in all areas at once. The progress happens gradually. Sue first started to keep her room clean, then her grades improved. Soon she offered to help around the house. It may take forever before Sue finds satisfaction in all virtues. If mature adults can't reach perfection in this life, how can a teenager? Maturity and a fulfilled ego as motivation are attained step by step.

In the meantime, most children need concrete rewards. An appropriate reward for two-year-old Jimmy might be that Mom reads a story to him or takes him to the store. Until your children accept abstract ego rewards, they will rely on others to reward them.

Rewards can be quite ordinary privileges for good behavior, such as meals on time or playing with a favorite toy. They can also be elaborate, such as ski vacations for good grades or allowance for good work.

Goals of Their Own

What happens when a child has no desire to act responsibly? You have waited and waited; you reward and extend privileges, but nothing motivates the child. She does not care to clean her room, do her chores, or clear her plate after dinner. This child would rather sit at the kitchen table all night in the dark than eat her green beans. You can still encourage these types of children to behave in a positive manner.

Spencer W. Kimball said, "I believe in goals, but I believe people should set their own." If nothing seems to motivate your child, find out what he likes to do. It may be something ludicrous. It may be something like getting 10,000 points on an Atari computer game. Whatever his goals are, find something that he can feel good about. Then motivate him accordingly.

When your child feels good about himself in one area, he will start to care about other areas. If Steve's friends start praising him because he's the only kid in the school who ever scored 10,000 points on a particular Atari game, Steve will start to wonder what his friends think about the way he combs his hair. He might wonder if they notice his grades. The key is to build self-confidence in your children.

Self-Esteem

Recently I met with a man who had been a school teacher and then a minister in Africa. While in Africa he had preached that we should "beware of wealth." One day he came upon a group of black children whose bellies were swollen with kwashiorkor and he thought, "It's terrible being poor. Because I am poor, I can't do anything to help these starving children." Then he made a deeply felt commitment to change. He decided he didn't want to be poor after all. With this commitment, he became a multimillionaire who could now help those less fortunate.

This man started with a burning commitment and then added a few successful experiences that is, he earned some money. From this success he gained a little self-esteem; then his self-esteem increased more and more. This very pleasant man developed an incredible amount of self-confidence. After what he accomplished, he deserved to feel good about himself.

The same thing could happen to your pimply-faced adolescent. But with girlfriends snubbing him and parents and siblings yelling at him, he experiences the antithesis of the success that the minister experienced. Instead, work to establish some successes that will encourage your adolescent to act responsibly in some way.

Parents are tempted to do just the opposite. They often join the pack of wolves baying at the adolescent's window.

Every time the youth makes a mistake, someone yells at him and hurts his self-esteem. The more people who yell, the worse off he gets. Stop the cycle. If you feel like yelling, find someplace else to yell. Go shout at the frogs on the lilies at the mill pond. Then sit down and talk with your child or teenager and encourage him to succeed in any area he possibly can.

The topic of self-esteem is worthy of a book all its own. Self-esteem gives a child strength to close his castle windows and avoid being vulnerable to archers' arrows. Although I can't cover the topic completely, I would like to briefly emphasize its importance in hopes that, if you are not doing so already, you will work to build self-esteem in your children.

Self-esteem is the strongest armor you can give a child to protect him from temptation. As your children enter an evil and corrupt world, they need self-esteem to combat adverse influences. Children who succumb to peers who introduce drugs, thievery, or promiscuity may lack confidence in themselves. It takes a strong child to say no. Young people must trust their own judgment as to what is right and wrong.

If children have been belittled in the home and have been taught that their opinions have no value, they may not believe in themselves outside the home. When a peer proposes an idea that conflicts with righteousness they may be easily persuaded to abandon appropriate teachings. Because saying no takes strength of character, a child who believes in himself will muster the courage to turn down temptation.

My wife has taught me a great deal about self-esteem. She considered it a great offense if one of the children called his brother or sister "stupid" or "dumb," and she provided immediate consequences. Negative, self-esteem – destroying words were not allowed in our home. Such words were seen as more damaging than even the physical abuse siblings tend to inflict.

Much recent research has documented the hazards of psychological child abuse. Although physical scars can heal, emotional wounds may never even develop a scab. Thus, the "sore-spot" remains open and vulnerable to tiny jabs, whether deliberate or not.

Parents, there are enough people who will tell your child that he's no good. Adolescents particularly are at a stage filled with self-doubt. At home your child deserves caring parents who reprove with love and spend the rest of their time helping him feel like he can conquer the world.

The self-fulfilled ego will guarantee appropriate behavior in an adolescent more often than parent-imposed consequences. Teens with self-fulfilled egos can provide their own rewards. When an adolescent sees intrinsic rewards in appropriate behavior, he will do what's right whether Mom and Dad are around or not.

6

Consequences:
Imposed and
Nonimposed

How many times have you heard a teen-
ager yell, "When I have kids, I'm never going to . . ." It would
be remarkable if your children felt so good about the way you
had reared them that they wanted to rear their own children
in precisely the same manner.

I hear teens complain about unfair punishments or the
consequences their parents provide for misbehavior as much
as any other aspect of parenting. When a consequence seems
unfair, a youth resists it.

The consequences included on the left side of the consequences continuum are chastisement, denying privileges,
and natural consequences. Chastisement may be considered
the opposite of praise, denying privileges the opposite of
rewards, and natural consequences the opposite of fulfilled
ego.

You may have noticed that spanking does not appear on
the continuum. This is because spanking is seldom, if ever, a
viable consequence for misbehavior. A swift swat may be a
way to get a child's attention when he is ignoring you or to

impress a one-year-old who's running into the street. But it doesn't teach children to abide by correct principles because they know the principles are true. It teaches children that when Mom and Dad are watching they'd better do what they have been told in order to avoid pain.

Other consequences make more sense than a punishment that inflicts pain. Pain may teach more anger and retaliation than awareness and remorse. Spanking is rarely a viable consequence and is seldom effective in permanently changing untoward behavior. As a punishment for hitting, you might separate the hitter from his playmate rather than spank him. Hitting a child only teaches the child to hit.

To stop his son's temper tantrum one father filled a cup with cold water and slowly poured it on the kicking child's head. The boy looked up in surprise, stopped crying, and never threw a temper tantrum again. I thought that was an original way to cool off a hothead.

Some parents find a brief spanking the easiest answer because the crying is over before long. But the really effective consequences require patience and persistence to administer. Your child would rather get a spanking and get it over with, just like you would, but other consequences will better remind the child not to repeat the error.

I imagine spanking came naturally to an angry Neanderthal parent who wanted to vent his feelings. Nevertheless, the purpose of a consequence is not to get even with a child. Consequences are to meet the needs of the individual child.

Chastisement

A "tongue lashing" or verbal reprimand should accompany virtually all misbehavior. Unless you tell a child what he did wrong and why, he may not even recognize his mistake.

Chapter 3 talks about chastisement as the first step in the repentance process. It also details the manner in which parents may chastise (reprove). There is a big difference between screaming and yelling in anger and helping a child recognize his mistake.

Often a verbal reprimand and parental disapproval is a severe enough consequence to bring about improved behavior. Sometimes, however, additional consequences may be necessary.

Proper chastisement is in effect a blessing for the child. Christ said, "He that will not bear chastisement is not worthy of my kingdom" (D&C 136:31). Nevertheless, even adults are not inclined to ask to be chastised.

Denying Privileges

When a child cannot act responsibly within his stewardship, rather than spank him you might want to tighten his pen. The most obvious way to tighten a child's pen is to take away some privileges.

If Billy acts impolite and throws a temper tantrum in front of company, remove him from polite company and send him to his bedroom.

Some pediatricians suggest that parents place a "hitter" in a playpen for two minutes. If he can climb out of the playpen, bring his car seat in the house and restrain him in the car seat for two minutes.

If the problem is a child who steals candy from the store, let the child pay for the candy and deny her the privilege of accompanying her friends to the store for some time.

If Stan gets bad grades in school, he might have to lose play time to find more time to study. Perhaps he might give up soccer or quit his after-school job.

When privileges are revoked that relate directly to the area in which the child was irresponsible, a child will be more likely to see justice in the punishment.

When taking away privileges, remember the value of a privilege varies with each individual child. Each child will respond in a unique manner to the same consequence. Becky may not care if Dad cuts off her allowance. Stuart might work diligently to earn it back. Just because Becky gets sent to her room for teasing does not mean Stuart should get sent to his room for teasing. Stuart might like being sent to his room!

How can you hand tailor a consequence to each circumstance and each child? It will help if you discuss the effective consequences with the child and then let your child provide the answer.

A Teaching Moment

The exclamations, "You're so dumb," "I hate you," and "That's not fair," may at times be warning signs that a consequence is unjust. When a child feels resentful about a consequence the punishment will not be effective. The child will not think he made a mistake, but will instead look for someone else to blame for his consequence. Usually a parent becomes the scapegoat.

To help children see justice in their punishment, talk to them. The word *discipline* comes from the word *disciple*. A disciple is a student of a teacher. Children are disciples in that they learn from their parents. When you discipline, it is as important to tell your child the reason for the consequence as it is to find the right consequence.

Parents who ask themselves, "Why am I imposing this consequence?" can avoid giving punishment without purpose. Then they can teach the child *why* he will receive a punishment. The child learns from the lesson, knows what he did wrong, and determines how to correct the mistake.

"You make me mad" sounds like retaliation rather than rehabilitation. "You will benefit from this lesson" sounds more like an opportunity to teach.

Ten-year-old Peter sat in his bedroom, contemplating his consequence and muttering to himself: "Dad always comes home late and Mom never has dinner ready on time. Dad was late for a meeting tonight and he yelled at Mom and she yelled at me, but what was it that I did? I don't even remember what I did. I'm not even sure what I'm in here for. I can't stop thinking of those dumb parents of mine who dump everything on me."

The same Peter could make the same mistake (whatever it was) and receive the same consequence and say to himself, "Mom and I had such fun shopping today, but when we came home, I blew it. I made a mistake and I'm sorry. I'm going to try hard not to do that again."

All children can respond like Peter did in the second situation if parents take the time to help the child understand why his consequence is appropriate for the particular misbehavior. The child can then commit to alter his behavior.

Optimally the child thinks, "I lost my privileges because I made a mistake. I'll not do that again, because I want my privileges back," rather than, "Mom got upset and took my privileges away; mean old Mom."

A district judge I observed sentenced a man to prison for five years. The judge belittled, severely reprimanded, and dehumanized the criminal, delivering his lecture in front of a crowded courtroom. Before the criminal left the courtroom I, as a psychiatrist, was asked to interview him. "I got a bum rap from a bad judge," the accused said. For thirty minutes he talked without once mentioning the behavior that brought him into the courtroom in the first place. This criminal went to prison for five years thinking about the injustice he received in court and wondering how he would get even with the judge. I doubt that during his five years in prison it will ever occur to him to make a commitment to change.

When children see their punishment as unjust, they too will blame the administrator of the punishment. No change will occur in their minds and no improvement in their behavior.

In some cases children will interpret a consequence as a reflection on their self-worth. A young child assumes that Mom and Dad always do what is right. He wants to behave perfectly, and when he receives a consequence for doing wrong he belittles himself. He feels his parents don't love him. Rather than motivate the child to improve, the consequence destroys the child's incentive to be a good person. His self-esteem is harmed to the point that he doesn't like himself enough to try to be a good person.

You can use a teaching moment to discuss the need for the consequence, and also to reassure the child that he is still a good person. You may not love his behavior, but you still love him—and he should know that.

Natural Consequences

Children who see the inevitable results of a mistake learn a powerful lesson. These results are called "natural consequences" because they occur regardless of what parents do. The natural consequences of misdeeds appear at the very end of the continuum because they are usually the most effective deterrent to repeating a misdeed.

"I told my nine-year-old to keep his bicycle out of the driveway at least once a day," Mr. Lewis told me. "A few weeks ago my wife backed the car out of the garage and smashed the bicycle beyond repair. I started to ground my son and send him to his room, but then I saw the distraught sadness on his face. I realized nothing I could do would affect him as much as the sight of his smashed bicycle and the knowledge that he would not have a bicycle to ride for a long time. After he earned enough money to buy a new bicycle, he kept it out of the driveway."

Years ago my little five-year-old cousin left the water running in her grandpa's kitchen. Somehow no one noticed until the water filled the sink, spilled over the counter, soaked the drawers, went onto the floor, ran all over the kitchen, and seeped into the basement. The water rained down upon a collection of her grandpa's journals, written in water-soluble ink, recording fourteen years of academic research.

Grandpa was the first to find the disaster. He called emphatically for help. Every nearby adult hurried to rescue his books, stop the water, and clean up the mess. After the critical moments passed, saintly, white-haired Grandpa found the little five-year-old girl watching the chaos. He walked with her into the kitchen where water surrounded their feet and said in a calm but firm voice, "Honey, we don't leave the water running when we are not in the room."

Decades later, when the little girl became a mother herself, she still recalled the incident with warm regard for her grandpa. She needed no other reprimand to teach her the lesson. The disaster itself provided punishment enough to encourage responsible habits.

Prevent Inquisitions and Trials

Natural consequences also help when you don't know who committed the crime. The "who dunnit?" game merely turns children into liars and sneaks.

Once I observed my neighbor watching his dog chase a car. The man ran into the house, got a newspaper, rolled it up, and called, "Here, Fido." Fido came, and my neighbor beat the dog for coming.

Parents figuratively "beat" their children for telling the truth.

"Did you take that money off my dresser?" Dad asks his child. When the child admits guilt, Dad punishes him. And parents wonder why children lie.

Children should not go on trial for every act. Parents do not need to act like prosecutor, judge, and jury. The home is not a court to determine guilt or innocence. Court trials teach children to "not get caught." Rather than putting their energy into behaving well, children put their energy into being sneaky. When parents hold trials children may reason thus: "If I plead guilty I'm sure to get five days in my room. If I plead innocent, no one will ever find out." Instead of confusing children by holding trials, let natural consequences provide the punishment.

Mrs. Jensen walked in the living room and saw her prized plant on its side. She knew if she held a trial to determine which child did it, she would hear, "Not me, not me." Like the Family Circus cartoon, an invisible ghost named "Nobody" would come to live at her house.

Instead of demanding to know who knocked over the plant, Mrs. Jensen cleaned it up. She made sure the children watched. They needed to know that whoever knocked over the plant inconvenienced Mother. Someone made a mistake. Someone should not have been running in the living room. It would be best if it did not happen again. Issue closed. Whoever "did it" knew not to do it again and was not tempted to lie.

The reason Mrs. Jensen might try to find out who did it would be to take out her anger on the child. That kind of punishment would not benefit the child as much as it would to watch Mother clean up the plant. Child-rearing does not have to be a trial for the children and a tribulation for the parents.

Overreacting

It's tempting, when trying to teach a child with natural consequences, to overreact to misbehavior. This shows the child that making messes (or whatever) really "gets to" the parent. When the child recognizes this, the child will use the mess making to control his parents.

I was raking the leaves one fall and conversing with my two-year-old son while he played in the leaves alongside me. I idly asked the boy, "What do you do when you are mad at Daddy?"

"I mess my pants," he responded frankly. The child's behavior was his way of saying, "This is how I express my negative feelings toward you."

Excessive punishment leads to negative feelings, negative feelings to negative behavior. This encourages more excessive consequences, and thus, more negative feelings and more negative behavior. Adults are responsible for having the understanding and insight necessary to break this cycle.

Developmentally, the average child cannot even accept responsibility for a mistake until his eighth year. (Precocious children may accept the responsibility for a mistake at age four, five, or six.) When I discovered this fact as a psychiatric resident, I was fascinated that child development experts had determined age eight as the year most children are fully accountable. Members of The Church of Jesus Christ of Latter-day Saints know the Lord established eight as the year a child is accountable and ready for baptism.

The researchers who arrived at this conclusion observed children who were given a set of preselected rules. Ninety-five percent of the children tested were able to follow the rules by the time they turned eight. My own observations agree.

Parents need not be distraught when a preschooler does not tell the truth, or when he takes something that does not belong to him, or when he breaks something. A "child-proof" house acknowledges the fact that small children do not have the capacity to tell themselves no. A parent who leaves Lladro porcelain on the coffee table with a toddler in the house is asking for broken Lladro.

It is possible to teach a two-year-old to stay away from china on the coffee table. Perhaps Mom and Dad spank his hands when he reaches for the china. Mom and Dad can train the two-year-old not to touch the glass, but they are not teaching him to be responsible. They are teaching him to be phobic. Like a dog, he won't touch the china for fear of being hit.

As we have discussed throughout this chapter, children develop at different rates. Children are not born responsible. Each child learns responsibility in a different area at a different age. Some children have more compliant personalities. And many children may be mature enough to accept responsibility long before age eight.

You may give your children an opportunity to accept responsibility and observe their progress. Gauge consequences according to their ability. In-home trials and excessive punishment lead the less mature child to lying, sneaking, and more untoward behavior.

Hope in Child-Rearing

Hope in child-rearing exists. Although you can't predict a child's behavior, you can stack the cards. You can become relatively certain that a child will respond to a consequence somewhere on the consequence continuum. When you discover what's important to your child, you can hand tailor the consequence accordingly. You who don't like to punish will be delighted when natural consequences prove successful.

As children learn to govern themselves they begin to recognize that there are consequences for everything they do; that is an inevitable part of life. Yet they will not really be free agents until they make the decisions that bring about desirable consequences.

7

How Children
Make Decisions

Mrs. Miller screamed at her preschool daughter, "Turn that television off." The little girl didn't hear so Mrs. Miller yelled louder. The toddler in the family walked in the room trailing a roll of toilet paper behind him and Mrs. Miller hollered again, this time so loud it frightened the child.

Soon Mrs. Miller's elderly mother called, "What should I do today, Mom?" she sweetly asked her mother. "Do you want me to finish that dress I'm making or should I read the book you brought over?"

Her mother said, "Read the book."

Mrs. Miller responded obediently, "Okay, Mom. Good idea."

That evening Mr. Miller came home from work and asked, "Do you remember the fireside we have to attend tonight, Sarah?"

"Are you conducting?"

"Yes."

"Then, I'm not going," she said rebelliously.

Four years ago Mr. Miller purchased a new house; in that time Mrs. Miller had still not decided what color to paint the kitchen. The basement was full of paint cans and the wall was covered with swatches, but Mrs. Miller couldn't make up her mind. When this woman took an axe to the baby grand piano, I hospitalized her.

This true story describes a woman who, in various situations, got stuck in each of the four stages of decision-making that children normally pass through.

The first stage, the "tyrant," is exemplified by the average two-year-old. The "puppet" stage is the "perfect angel" stage, which generally is achieved by the child around ten years old. The "rebel" predominates sometime during adolescence, and the "conflicted" stage appears in young adulthood before becoming a mature, independent, thinking adult. Often these stages are delayed: I've seen the rebellion stage occur into a person's forty's and fifty's.

Mrs. Miller got hung up at not one but all of these stages.

Your children make decisions at each of these stages throughout their youth. Sometimes ten-year-olds make decisions like tyrants and some two-year-olds make decisions like rebels. In some situations, even mature adults make decisions at one of these less mature stages.

Parents can encourage developmental arrest without even knowing it, causing their children to develop the personality of a puppet, tyrant, or rebel. The rest of this chapter will help you recognize these stages. As you become aware of the potential pitfalls, you can avoid them.

The Tyrant

If Bryce doesn't get candy before dinner he screams as long as he possibly can. If he doesn't want to get in the car to go to church, he plays "rag doll" and falls on the floor, refusing to move. If Bryce doesn't get his way on the playground, he takes the ball and runs home. Before he was big enough to run he tried to manipulate people by saying, "If you don't play with me I won't be your friend."

Two-year-olds are notorious for this type of an I-want-what-I-want-when-I-want-it attitude. They have temper tantrums until they get what they want.

If the whole world were to make their decisions on the basis of what they want and what they feel like, could you imagine how many accidents would occur in intersections? Everybody would want to go through the light at the same time.

People who make decisions based solely on what they want are tyrants. Those whom you may call strong-willed may actually be strong "want" and strong "feel like" people. They can't resist their own desires and they must have their own way.

The Puppet

Fortunately, someone helps control the two-year-old within each child: his parents. Parents say, "You ought to eat your vegetables before you eat dessert," or "You should clean up your room before you go out to play."

Everybody needs a good parent who can help him control the two-year-old inside him. When parents go away, children need to listen to the parental voice within them.

A parental voice speaks in my head. When I go to the hospital cafeteria and go through the lunch line, I see cottage cheese and tomatoes and also cottage cheese and pineapple. The voice in my head says, "Son, eat your tomatoes, they're good for you."

And I say, "But Mom, I'd rather have pineapple."

The voice says, "Sorry son, the pineapple's all blockaded by the Japanese in Pearl Harbor." (That tells you how old I am—that mental tape recording is at least forty years old. In fact they didn't even have tape in those days; it was steel wire.)

However, I still go through the cafeteria line choosing tomatoes. I don't even like tomatoes.

One day I took my son to McDonald's and he started to pull the tomato out of his hamburger. I asked him, "What are you doing that for?"

"I don't like tomatoes," he said.

"I don't like them either," I said, "but I eat them anyway."

"That's dumb," he replied.

In some respects, he was right. The "oughts" and "shoulds" that my parents taught me to help me be a "perfect angel" still remain in my mind. However, boys and girls who follow every ought and should in their heads can make decisions like puppets. Too often they are governed entirely by these oughts and shoulds that their parents taught them, and they can't make a decision on their own.

Parents can teach their children what's right and raise very good children. However, if the children behave like perfect angels only because Mom and Dad still control the puppet strings they will not attain true perfection. True perfection requires that each man exercise his free agency and make decisions on his own.

I often hear little boys playing. "What do you want to do?" one asks. "Oh, I don't know. What do you want to do?"

The little boy is truly at a loss to make a decision independent of an ought-should tape recording in his head.

In the movie *Marty*, Ernest Borgnine stands on a street corner in New Jersey. For five minutes he and his buddy, both thirty-five-year-old bachelors, try to decide what to do. They talk for so long without making a decision that the audience all goes out to buy popcorn.

Most children behave like perfect angels when they are around ten years old. Those who teach fifth grade know what I mean. Ten is a delightful age. The majority of the kids know how to behave. The teacher can go down to the principal's office and say, "Class, I'm going to be gone for a minute. Behave yourselves."

When she returns one or two of the students may have thrown spitwads, but the majority are working in their workbooks. Ten-year-olds know how to do what their elders tell them to do.

The problem is that a "perfect angel" may do what he ought to do and should do most of the time, but when around poor companions he is as easily influenced by them as by his parents. He often acts like a puppet. During adolescence he is exceptionally vulnerable to peer exploitation.

The story of Pinocchio tells how a literal wooden puppet was drawn into the evil Stromboli's clutches because he listened to the persuasions of a sly fox. A child who makes decisions at the puppet stage is easily persuaded to misbehave. When his parents leave town and are not near to tell him what to do, watch out for the parties he attends.

Fortunately, only chimpanzees are mature at age ten. Humans continue to grow up a lot after ten years of age. If an adult makes all his decisions like a ten-year-old, he is no more than a puppet. He listens to the oughts and shoulds his parents taught him, but he doesn't learn to make decisions for himself. He is arrested at the puppet stage where oughts and shoulds cause him to be ashamed, guilty, or embarrassed at what people might think when he goes against his parents' wishes.

The Rebel

When a ten-year-old grows older he may, at one time, sneak behind the barn to smoke a cigar. He does not necessarily "want" to smoke a cigar. (At least not the first time.) However, if he feels he's old enough to make his own decisions regarding tobacco and he's been told not to smoke cigars, what's the other decision he might make in an effort to be independent?

The rebel represents the third stage of decision-making.

He does the opposite of what he is told, just to declare his independence. If Mother says "wear your hair longer," he cuts it. If she wants him to cut it, he grows it longer.

Rebellion causes much of the bad behavior adults see after ten years of age. Parents often complain about adolescent rebellion. You wish it would go away—and it will sooner rather than later with parental understanding. It is an inevitable stage of development.

The Child in Conflict

Virtually every adolescent wakes up one Saturday morning and says to herself, "What a mess I left on this floor. Look at the dresser; I think I'm going to clean up my room before I go over to visit my friend."

Then Mother comes down the hall and yells, "Before you go over to visit your friend, be sure to clean up your room."

There goes her motivation. If she cleans the room now she will feel she did it only because Mom said to. But if she doesn't clean it up when she had already made the decision she was going to clean it up, who got her to change her mind? Mom. So the adolescent lies in bed feeling caught.

There are even adults who find themselves caught between what they want to do and what they should do.

"I ought to go to church this morning . . .

"but I don't want to go to church . . .

"but I should go . . .

"but I don't feel like it . . .

"but I promised the bishop I'd go. . . ."

What happens to church attendance when an individual has a fight in his head? How well will you sleep in on Sunday morning knowing you should be at church?

Conflicts between what a person ought to do and what she wants to do may not always cover big issues, but like a little rock right under the oil pan, they can high-center the adolescent. Unresolved decisions can be extremely debilitating. People can get headaches and neck aches, stomach aches, back aches, ulcers, asthma, fears, phobias, depression, and all kinds of psychosomatic ills from unresolved conflicts. They're caught between the rock of wants and feelings and the hard place of oughts and shoulds.

Sometimes a bright teenager will recognize when he gets stuck at the conflicted stage of decision-making. A mother brought her daughter into my office, worried that the daughter hated her.

"My daughter won't do the dishes or anything if I'm the one to ask her."

"I don't mind doing the dishes," the daughter said. "I usually plan to do them—until you come in and start bossing me around."

"Why don't you do them anyway?" asked the mother.

"You destroy my motivation. I don't like you to tell me everything I'm supposed to do. I can think for myself. I know when the dishes need to be cleaned. When you interrupt me, I don't know whether to do them because they're dirty or to leave them to show you that I can be my own boss."

Decisions at All Four Levels

Remember the story of Mrs. Miller, who made various decisions at all four levels? With her children she behaved like a tyrant; with her mother like a puppet; with her husband she was a rebel; and through it all she made extremely conflicted decisions.

Few children will take an ax to a baby grand piano, but watch an adolescent undergo mood changes. They rebel and do the opposite of what you ask one day, and they obey the rules without question on the next. They are experimenting with various stages of decision-making.

Creating a Tyrant

Without even knowing it, parents can train their children to think like tyrants. To raise a tyrant, take a two-year-old to the grocery store and put him in the cart while you shop. When he gets in front of the candy you can be almost certain he'll say, "Mama, I'm tired of fruits and vegetables, buy me a candy bar or I'll have a temper tantrum."

If you buy him a candy bar every time you go to the store, who will run your life?

Creating a Puppet

Let me tell you how parents raise puppets. They say to a child, "Young man, as long as you live in this house we'll make your decisions for you. We pay for the roof over your head, the clothes on your back, the food on your table. Therefore we'll make all your decisions (and put you in an undersized pen) until your eighteenth birthday, and then you must make your own decisions (and instantly be put in an adult-sized pen). You must decide if you'll go to college or join the army." How is an adolescent to make these "little" decisions when he has rarely experienced decision-making?

Another tactic also creates puppets. Can you hear a mother say, "After all we have done for you and you're not going to do what I say? You'll be the death of me yet!"

Parents who accuse a child of murder hold a pretty strong handle on his strings. It is easy to see why some adolescents are easily influenced when they function as puppets, even after they become adults.

Creating a Rebel

So you want to raise a rebel? The more you fight them, the more rebellious teens become. Adolescent rebellion can occur traumatically or graciously. The more gracious the rebellion and the sooner the adolescent gets over it, the better off he is. If you can facilitate the child in getting through rebellion, things will get better.

If you refrain from interfering, soon the child who goes behind the barn to smoke a cigar will recognize that "he who smokes the cigar smells the most smoke." An adolescent eventually learns that rebellion is dumb because he is still not in charge of himself. If he makes decisions based on the *opposite* of what somebody told him he is still basing his decision on their opinion. You may share this thought with an adolescent to help him outgrow the rebellion stage.

Best Decisions

Suppose your teenager got up one morning and wanted a glass of milk. She went to the refrigerator, but there was only enough milk for one glass and you had a two-year-old house guest. She could hear the two-year-old stirring in the back room. If she drank the milk it would not be illegal, immoral, or fattening (as long as it was not whole milk). It would not necessarily be a *bad* decision for her to drink it. However, if the two-year-old hadn't had his milk yet, it wouldn't be the *best* decision for her to drink that milk. If she said no to her desire to drink that milk because her mother wouldn't like it, that reflects on the mother's maturity. If it is the adolescent's decision because she has considered the two-year-old and decided what would be best, she knows how to make a *best* decision.

Naturally, children mature more quickly in some areas than in others. Part of the "one step forward, two steps back" growth process includes becoming mature in one area at a time. One father shared this situation:

"Judy, our kindergarten daughter, acted very grown up when her cousins came for the holidays. She volunteered to give up her room and shared her best Barbie dolls willingly. I thought she was acting so mature. The arguments began . when the cousins started discussing Superman. 'He can too stop time,' my daughter insisted. 'He can do anything in the world.' Her cousins disagreed and Judy would not give in. She would not even consider the fact that her cousin might have a different opinion. I realized that though Judy could share her possessions, she lacked maturity when it came to accepting a viewpoint different than her own."

The individual who overcomes the childish stages of decision-making can make *best* decisions. I define a *best* decision as the most effective solution, arrived at independently.

Best decisions obey the golden rule. *Best* decisions provide their own reward. The child who makes *best* decisions can say no to tempting friends or meddlesome parents and also to selfish wants and "feel likes."

Independent Decisions

Unfortunately a lot of people besides you, as mother and father, try to tell your children what they "ought" to do. Those people don't agree either. Your children can't keep everybody happy. One company says, "I'd be happy if you'd drink Sprite," while the other says, "I'd be happy if you'd drink 7-Up."

Your children often receive diametrically opposed bits of advice. Your children can get caught trying to keep everyone happy. The best thing is for people to control their own lives. They can learn to make *best* decisions within their own pens. They can take advice from their feelings, and advice from the oughts and shoulds in their heads, but ultimately they must make a *best* decision on their own.

A parental voice does not need to create a puppet. Even young children may learn to listen to the parental voice, consider the advice, and control their wants and feelings. This means they will resist selfish impulses and then make independent, *best* decisions within their own stewardship.

Best Decisions

8

Not the Parents' Decision

It's easy to let your children make their own decisions when they make the decision you suggest. But sometimes children will not follow these "oughts" and "shoulds" in their stewardships that are truly good advice.

In order to make their own decisions in their stewardships, children must say no to some of the people telling them what they ought to and should do. Some advice-givers do not have the children's best interests at heart. As your child grows older he eventually learns to tell his parents no regarding matters within his stewardship. (Children often outgrow their parents when they study computers, for instance.) It is the chick that must crack the egg, not the chicken.

Tragedy may occur if your children do not learn to say no when appropriate. What if your daughter parks on a hillside with a boyfriend while looking down at a sunset. Suppose that you've done a thorough job of teaching her to be a good ten-year-old puppet who says, "Yes Mama, yes Daddy, okay." What will happen when the fellow puts his arm around her and says, "If you love me you'll give me a little kiss"? When her response comes out a timid, miscommunicating, "Nooo, dooon't!" that girl's likely to get kissed (and then some) whether she wants to be kissed or not.

A fifteen-year-old girl sat on my couch in her third trimester explaining that she had become pregnant because her boyfriend had started to cry. Perfect angels don't ever hurt people's feelings, do they? Frankly, when I hear that anyone over twelve is a "perfect angel," I am concerned that they are vulnerable to exploitation. Developmentally, a period of rebellion is still likely.

Teaching children to say the actual word *no* when within their stewardship, even at the risk of hurting someone's feelings or going against someone's wishes, is a most important, protective goal. The right to say no is essential in making decisions. For instance, How would you feel if your son went to the front door one day and saw a fellow selling magazines. In an effort to get your son to buy the magazines this fellow said, "Come on, buy the magazines. Don't you want me to get to go to college?" along with a few other manipulative phrases. Your son responds, "I appreciate the opportunity to buy your magazines, but we have all the magazines we need; the answer is no." You would be proud of your son. He protected your pocketbook. He respects the allowance you give him and wants to use it carefully.

Your son deserves the same privilege of saying no to you when making decisions within his stewardship as he does of saying no to the salesman. If your son manages his responsibilities, he has the privilege of saying no regarding those matters in which he has shown the maturity to handle himself. This privilege may make him less vulnerable to manipulation (including yours) than he was in the past. The decisions allocated to your son are his to make, no one else's.

The oughts and shoulds that come from parents must not completely dictate their children's behavior. If children work within their stewardship the parents' oughts and shoulds will serve only as advice. If Mother comes up to her twenty-two-year-old son and says, "I think you should major in engineering," he may say, "Mom, I appreciate your advice; I have considered that. But right now I will declare my major as business." Part of parental growth, although a struggle, is learning to accept this independent decision-making.

I saw a dear fifty-year-old lady who came in to my office regarding her seventeen-year-old daughter. This rather rebellious daughter caused all kinds of problems. In the course of our conversation, the mother told me about going to the mall and buying some fabric with her seventy-five-year-old mother.

"How did Grandma handle that?" I asked.

"I started to buy some material," she said, "but Grandma saw the fabric and said, 'I don't like that color,' so I didn't buy it."

"How would your daughter act if you told her you didn't like the fabric?"

"That's the trouble, doctor. My daughter would have bought it anyway."

The fifty-year-old mother, a puppet, let a seventy-five-year-old grandmother, a tyrant, run her life and thought she should run her seemingly rebellious seventeen-year-old daughter's life the same way. The seventeen-year-old was more mature than the mother or the grandmother.

Allowing Small Children to Make Decisions

Young children will not receive as many opportunities to make their own decisions as teenagers, because they live in smaller pens. However, you can still allow children responsibility within their own stewardship. You need not wait until children are ten years old to give them responsibilities. As we discussed in chapter 2, as a child develops his ability within his crib, he chooses his own rattles. No one climbs in his crib and chooses his rattles for him (unless he's breaking them and eating the pieces). The child should choose his own rattles. When he's in the backyard playing in the sandbox, he can choose his toys.

I sat at a dinner table one day discussing this very topic with a friend of mine from the military. This captain sat with his two young children while he watched my son (two and a half years old) climb up on the chair across the table. My son then started to put his hand in the candle that sat on the table. What do you do when a toddler goes to put his hand in a candle? Most people would grab him, but I didn't.

I turned to the captain and said, "I will teach this young man correct principles and then let him govern himself." This is the same principle Joseph Smith used in governing the Saints in the early days of the Church. I said to my son, "If you put your hand in that candle you'll burn yourself; candles are hot." He put his hand right in the candle. Of course, the candle was hot enough to reinforce my point but not so hot as to damage the child's hand permanently.

In this case my son learned two very important lessons: (1) candles are hot, and (2) Dad gives good advice. The latter lesson is probably the more important lesson to learn, particularly at age two rather than as a teenager. The sooner the boy can keep his hands out of candles, the better off he will be—as he grows older, the candles get bigger and hotter.

Remember there is obviously a limit to the freedoms you can give a two-year-old, even to teach him a lesson. Now, if I had removed my son but left the candle on the table and then left the room, my son would have gone right back to that candle and would probably have burned the house down. Neither would I have used a roaring fireplace or a hot stove to teach the lesson. We don't allow children to experience the risk of permanent damage. The mother I spoke of in the introduction to this book allowed a mousetrap to teach her child the very important lesson that parents give good advice. It is an exceptional parent who can thus relinquish control.

If parents allow a child to make his own decisions within his stewardship, he will learn how to make decisions. When he grows up and Mom and Dad live too far away to make decisions for him, he will know how to make *best* decisions. By then the boy will be an expert at decision-making. He will have long ago graduated from the unhealthy decision-making stages and will now make *best* decisions on his own.

Somewhere in between the tyrant (who lets wants make his decisions) and the puppet (who lets oughts and shoulds make decisions for him) lie *best* decisions. The mature decision-maker considers his feelings and wants in one ear, the oughts and shoulds in the other ear, then makes an independent decision based on what is best.

9

Too Grown Up for Mom and Dad

When children become adolescents they have to make some very big decisions on their own. Because when they encounter these situations what they want may be a stronger influence than what they ought, parents hope that their children will have learned to make *best* decisions.

I have included this chapter on chastity because I have seen numerous youth who felt unprepared to make a *best* decision in this area. And I've counseled as many parents who felt helpless when teaching their youth the reasons why fidelity is best.

Once when I was on my way to deliver a lecture on this subject, I saw an incredible sight. I looked up in the sky towards the state capitol, and just above the copper dome I saw what looked like an airplane on fire. Cars were stopping along the road to see what was happening.

It was a little bit awesome to think that somebody was up there in an airplane that was on fire. I could see pieces falling off and burning and I wondered what was really happening.

Suddenly I realized that the fire ball was a satellite re-entering the atmosphere. The Statue of Liberty on the Fourth of July couldn't have offered more fascination, and the fireworks appeared just as spectacular. Pieces of the satellite broke off and burned out like a sparkler.

Once I understood what was happening, I enjoyed the scene. When I understood that no harm was coming to me or anyone else, it was quite beautiful. When I didn't understand what was happening, I was quite anxious.

The same thing happens to adolescents as they discover sexual intercourse. The experience can be devastating when it's not under control, and beautiful when it is appropriate and legitimate.

You may find it difficult to discuss this topic with your adolescent because sex involves some strong feelings that are hard to put into words. Because feelings are difficult to express, sometimes parents and teens are unable to communicate on the topic of sex.

When trying to communicate with your adolescents, encourage them to give you feedback. Their perception of sex may be entirely different than yours. Feedback will help you both know when understanding occurs.

One of the reasons misunderstandings occur when talking about sex is that the same event can affect you and your teen in a completely different way. In fact the very same words describing sex can mean one thing to you and something else to your teen.

The misperceptions people have when a word has two different meanings are similar to the misperceptions you and your teen may have when the same event has two different meanings.

Words with Two Meanings

A professor at a local university once related this message to me. If your daughter were at a football game and saw her boyfriend catch a pass and run into the end zone she might exclaim with her hands clasped over her heart, "What a man!"

When a woman runs all over the house picking up her husband's dirty socks she might also exclaim (with both hands resting on her hips), "What a man."

The lonely old woman who looks under her bed and sees someone of the male gender might raise her arms in the air and yell, "What, a man?"

All three women use the exact same words but each means something entirely different.

One mother illustrated this point when she told me about her daughter's first visit to church. "Did you hear that man?" the little girl asked. "He swore right in front of everybody."

"I didn't hear him swear," the mother said.

"Yes, Momma. He said, *G-o-d*."

This mother explained that people use the same words in prayer that people use when they are profaning. People can use words either in a good or a bad way.

The same words that describe appropriate marital affection can be used inappropriately to express vulgarity. The words themselves are not good or bad. The words are merely symbols. They are just scribbles on paper or noises in the air. The value or meaning attached to the symbols determines whether they are good or bad.

Behavior with Two Meanings

A handshake is a lot like a word with two meanings. When you meet someone you haven't seen for a long time you each throw out a hand. There's no gun in it; there's no knife in it; there's not a clenched fist. What's your message?

You are saying, "Hello, friend, I'm glad to see you."

If somebody extends a hand that feels like a wet fish, you might wish you didn't have to take it. Or you might not see them extend the hand and you might walk right on by. That's embarrassing and I would hope nobody notices. An empty handshake is no fun. Handshakes are meant to be shared and mutually enjoyed.

I don't know anybody (unless it's a politician) that counts the number of handshakes he receives in a day. Handshakes are meant to be given enthusiastically and warmly by both parties. They are not as much fun when one person is not eager to greet the other.

The same thing happens with hugs. People don't keep a journal to write down the number of hugs they receive each day. Hugs are gifts, not "gets," that people exchange with one another.

We give handshakes to people we are happy to meet; we give hugs to good friends and relatives; we give kisses to Mom, Dad, close relatives, and perhaps other loved ones; and we give intercourse only to a legally married husband or wife as the most intimate expression of affection.

Marital relations are a gift. They are a gift within a marriage. Sex is an expression of mutual affection between a husband and a wife.

Some people who are not mature may want to "get" more than they give. Sometimes even within a marriage sexual intercourse is used not as a gift but as an exploitation.

Sex without commitment is frequently used by couples as a form of mutual self-stimulation. Sometimes it is used to take advantage of one another and to meet an individual need. Often marital relations are used by one spouse to manipulate the other. In this case marital relations are used as a control mechanism or even prostitution within a marriage. At the very worst, sex can be used to express hostility, even abuse and rape.

Teenagers need to know the ramifications of sexual relations because the media romanticizes and exploits sex and often does not paint an accurate picture.

When teens understand the consequences and results of sex, they can plan and prepare to make it a beautiful experience—as was the burning satellite when I understood it.

As we teach youth appropriate sexual behavior we need to be careful about our choice of words and the meaning our children apply to those words. Sexual behavior is not dirty or bad any more than words are dirty or bad. But the message may be bad if the behavior is illegal, abusive, or exploitive. Sexual behavior, like driving a car, is not wrong or bad if (1) you have a valid marriage license, (2) you are considerate, and (3) you are responsible and committed.

The Physical Consequences of Sex

The primary purpose of sex is to create people. (Affection and bonding is a secondary purpose.) If there wasn't any sex there wouldn't be any people. For that matter, there wouldn't be any other creatures either.

Your children would benefit from an understanding of the process called procreation. Sex is a species need as well as an individual need. It is also an individual privilege that requires responsibility.

How would your twelve-year-old son or daughter feel if they were driving down the street and saw a car coming toward them that was driven by one of their classmates in school? Before they would feel comfortable about their buddies driving they would want to make sure that he was old enough, that he had taken driver's education, and that he had a driver's license. Then they could feel safer on the road. (However, it is not essential to diagram a carburetor to know how to drive. Some proposed sex-education classes are like advanced auto mechanics courses rather than driver's education programs.) The driver must understand and obey the traffic rules and drive responsibly with a license.

Adolescents should likewise contemplate a responsible sexual partner, one who understands and obeys the interpersonal rules of respect. Those rules include marriage as being prerequisite to sexual relations. A marriage partner must be old enough for trust and commitment and have a marriage license.

One of the saddest consequences of premature sex is a loss of trust. Even married people who started sexual behavior too soon later wonder, "If we couldn't say no to each other premaritally, how can we be sure we will say no to others extramaritally?" Such distrust brings couples into my office for marriage counseling.

One of the greatest experiences that can happen to a man and his wife is to have a baby. It is a great joy to have a baby come into a home that eagerly awaits its arrival. In contrast, one of the saddest things is for a baby to come into a home that does not have a mother and father who are committed to each other and who have the commitment and ability to care for a baby.

As a child-psychiatrist I am often involved with children who come into this world to parents who do not care about them. In many of these cases, the children are a result of premarital sexual relations and the parents were not ready to be a mother or father.

There are many ways of avoiding pregnancy, but I would suggest you teach your children a proven method that can prevent both unwanted pregnancy and damaging emotional scars.

The best way to avoid premarital sex is to say *no!* Teach your adolescents to say, "I can and I will wait until I am married." The other methods of birth control work a percentage of the time but only one method works 100 percent of the time.

Your adolescents will find it difficult to say no to intercourse unless they also say no to petting. A canoe drifting down a river is easy to steer when the waters are calm. As the canoe approaches the rapids that lead to the falls it becomes more and more difficult to paddle away from the falls.

People on a diet shouldn't loiter in the kitchen where the pies are baking; such self-temptation is foolish. Petting is the same as foreplay, which belongs to marriage. It is a part of sexual affection. A youth who paddles too close to the falls is too easily pulled over a mighty steep drop.

Diseases

Venereal disease used to be one of the things people who engaged in premarital sex feared the most. Nobody knows where venereal disease started, but evidence of the disease can be found in the tombs of Egypt. It appears that the disease has been around as long as people have been making mistakes.

You can explain the different types of venereal diseases to your children. Gonorrhea is an infection that affects the genital urinary system and can cause a puslike infection much like a bad pimple. It has a discharge and causes a great deal of pain.

Gonorrhea used to be treated successfully with penicillin, however the bacteria are becoming immune to penicillin and the disease is now more difficult to treat. Permanent sterility is the most tragic consequence of gonorrhea.

Syphillis is more dangerous and more difficult to treat in late stages. It starts out as an infection on the skin and eventually infects the entire body, finally affecting the nervous system, including the brain. Thirty years ago, a large number of the patients in the mental hospitals were there because they had syphillis that could not be treated successfully.

Herpes is a viral infection that is related to cold sores, but is contracted only through genital contact. Because antibiotics do not affect viruses it cannot be cured. Although there are treatments for the symptoms, the only way to treat the disease is to let it die out—with the person who contacted it.

AIDS (Acquired Immune Deficiency Syndrome) is the most horrible disease that can be contracted through illicit sexual intercourse. Although the majority of AIDS victims are homosexuals, bisexuals have now spread AIDS into the heterosexual community. Those who died of AIDS as a result of a blood transfusion were fewer than 10 percent of AIDS victims.

AIDS is a disease that affects the body's immune system. The victim cannot ward off any disease and will die of anything from strep throat to encephalitis. It acts inexorably and is mercilessly cruel.

One woman who died of AIDS a week after an interview with *USA Today* said, "I never, never, never, never thought I'd get AIDS." Although condoms can decrease the chance of AIDS (some researchers think they prevent it), the most sure way your child can avoid contracting the disease is to say, "no!" He or she must avoid premarital sexual intercourse or any perversions thereof to remain completely safe.

Psychological Ramifications

When an unmarried man and unmarried woman experience sex and think they are expressing love, it can be very hard on their feelings when they discover it wasn't love at all.

Such sexual encounters are like having a friend that pretends to be your friend only so you can do him a favor, such as taking him on a skiing trip. As soon as you've taken him skiing he drops you. When your adolescent gets dropped from the most intimate of affectionate relationships, it can be a very painful experience.

I once saw a cartoon that I'll never forget. I tend to forget cartoons after a chuckle, but this particular cartoon did not make me chuckle—it made me very sad. In the first picture there was a little boy about eight years old and below him his dad was yelling, "Jump, Haime, Jump." In the second frame it showed little Haime jumping into the air with total trust. In the third picture little Haime lay flat on the ground. Underneath the cartoon the caption read, "That will teach you not to trust anybody." After I saw that cartoon I felt sick. It is a very unfortunate situation to trust somebody and have them break that trust.

Your children will develop little friendships with their schoolmates, and when one of those friends they play with breaks their trust it will hurt their feelings a little bit. When people develop relationships based on a lot of intimacy and a lot of trust they become vulnerable to a lot of pain.

When two people enter into a sexual relationship and one of the partners in the relationship breaks the trust by developing a relationship with someone else or simply abandoning his partner, it destroys trust.

I have seen people that suffer for years after an intimate relationship ended. The hurt they feel often prevents them from ever trusting someone else enough to develop an intimate, loving relationship.

When one partner in a sexual relationship has saved such affection for marriage and the other has not, distrust can occur. Even when the couple has never had a sexual relationship except a premarital relationship with one another, they may develop a mutual distrust.

In the previous chapter you learned how to teach your children to say no. They will have the courage to say no to sexual intimacy prior to marriage if this lesson has been well taught.

Breaking the Habit

Adolescents who have difficulty saying no to sex may have had difficulty saying no to themselves as children.

As a newborn baby lies on his back he begins to see his fingers and toes for the first time. He will hold his fingers up to the light and explore his hand, and then he will bring his foot to his face and play with his toes.

As the baby boy grows bigger he is able to sit up, and when he sits in the bathtub he can see his genital area. He expresses curiosity about this area just like he does the rest of his body. It's important that the baby learn about his anatomy.

When the child grows older and starts to play with himself Mom and Dad teach him that his penis is for going to the bathroom and not for playing with. He learns not to play with himself and he puts on his pants. By the time children are four or five they generally have learned not to play with themselves.

Around eleven or twelve years of age young men start playing with themselves again. At this age, playing with one's genitalia for the purpose of self-stimulation is masturbation.

The body is designed for a certain purpose—and it works —but when abused there are psychological ramifications. For instance, your pediatrician has probably shown you the growth curves that measure a child's height and weight. There is also a curve for emotional development that I call the "Can you take it?" curve. This curve measures a child's ability to handle stress.

A little boy who is only eight years old when he has a shot of heroin learns the effect of that substance on his mind. Then, when he gets to be fourteen and his mother runs off, his dad goes to prison, he flunks out of school, and his girlfriend drops him, he remembers that heroin can alter a depressed mental state.

Early in life this little boy found heroin desirable and he relied on it as the stresses increased. He did not develop the natural ability to deal with stress, but became addicted to the drug to anesthetize his pain. Other drugs such as cocaine,

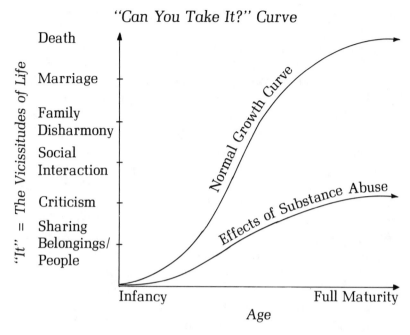

"Can You Take It?" Curve

barbituates, alcohol, tobacco, and marijuana can be abused the same way.

Just as drugs and alcohol can become addicting, the sexual experience has an addictive effect. Physically, masturbation doesn't cause hair to grow on a boy's palms nor does it cause other physical changes; however, it can alter a boy's mind as he uses masturbation to deal with feelings. He can create an artificial feeling of well-being instead of effectively dealing with his problems and stresses.

When this little boy meets a girl who can gratify him even more than the masturbation, their relationship becomes a matter of self-gratification. Rather than masturbating, boys would better deal with their feelings by talking to a parent or a counselor who can help.

A young girl often becomes pregnant when she has premature sexual relations because, like watching the burning satellite, she does not fully understand what she is experiencing.

Most young girls do not plan to have premarital sexual relations, but as they mature they experience feelings they have not felt before. When a girl finds herself in an affectionate situation that she is not familiar with, she might not know how to thwart impending intimacy.

To protect your sons and daughters from such unfamiliar situations, you might encourage them to keep three rules: early hours, lots of people, and lots of light. Few people will become sexually intimate when there are other people around or when it's light.

Our promiscuous society has made it illegal to teach sexual morals in the schools. Many educators assume or even advocate premarital sexual relations. Then after the forest is in flames they provide a fire engine to put out the fire and assume birth control devices will stop pregnancy.

As a child-psychiatrist, regardless of the theological morals of my patients, I encourage sexual relations only within marriage because too many people get "burned" by premarital sexual relations, and the scars last a lifetime. And they burden marriage and child-rearing ability.

Adolescents sometimes think they are "too grown up for Mom and Dad." Intent on becoming independent, communication becomes difficult as adolescents consider rebellion. Hopefully, the child will have tried rebellion at age two. They will remember experimenting with mousetraps and birthday candles the lesson they learned: parents give good advice.

When the principles regarding stewardship and decisions are applied, they enable adolescents to make responsible behavior their own choice.

The issues of alcohol, drugs, and sexual relations do not daunt the adolescent who can make *best* decisions. They are responsible stewards, having been taught tried and true principles.

"I raise my children as I would my most gifted ball players," a football coach once told me. Once the game begins the quarterback can call an audible whenever he wants. A well-executed play is the sign of good coaching. Parenting is a lot like good coaching.

10

Areas of
Decision-Making

When you think of decision-making you may picture yourself selecting one of Baskin Robbins's thirty-one flavors. Selecting a flavor of ice cream represents a well-known type of decision: a decision regarding behavior.

Everybody makes decisions regarding behavior. Your behavior is a tangible act. Decisions regarding behavior may include whether to watch television or play ball in the backyard; whether to go out dancing or go to bed early. Children decide if they want to go to the store with Mother or mow the lawn with Father; they decide whether they want to wear pants or shorts, a blue shirt or a red one; whether to behave or misbehave.

People make decisions in several other areas that they do not recognize as easily as decisions regarding behavior. In fact, your children may not even know they can make decisions in these other areas. The other areas of decision-making include decisions of attitude, thinking, and feeling. These decisions do not deal with behavior; they deal with thought.

Each of these decisions regarding thought differs greatly from the other. Your children can recognize their ability to make decisions regarding attitude, thinking, and feeling. Then they can make deliberate decisions rather than being controlled by their habits of attitudes, thinking, or feelings.

Decisions of Attitude

A fashion model stomped out of her photo session. "That's just the way I am. Like it or leave it," she said. "I cannot help it if I look like I'm pouting." Many adults refuse to change because they think, "That's just the way I am." Children and adolescents can learn early that they have the ability to change their attitudes.

In the movie *Footloose*, a group of high school seniors changed their attitude toward the slick kid from Chicago who wore skinny ties and combed his hair askew. The Chicago kid likewise erased his preconceived notions that small country towns were backward. Their decision to change their attitudes enabled them to all enjoy one another and become friends.

You may know children who will not try new games. "It will be dumb," they say. One five-year-old girl refused to invite anyone to her birthday party. "No one likes parties anyway, Mom," she said. Adults readily recognize children with an "attitude problem." Adolescents particularly are accused of "having a bad attitude." Yet they can make a conscious decision to change their attitudes.

An attitude is a state of mind you establish. Children can decide what type of attitude they will have before they ever encounter a situation. Children can learn to enjoy ball games even if they don't win. Before they ever start to play, teach them to have a positive attitude even if the other team wins.

Salespeople can teach your children a great deal about attitude. If a real estate saleswoman brought someone in to see a home she had listed and thought, "I never make any sales. There's no way these people will buy this house," she wouldn't be a saleswoman for long. If your child knocks on all your neighbor's doors trying to sell chocolate bars, he'd better learn to remain happy even if no one purchases his candy bars.

Situations need not determine attitudes. Handicapped people don't have to feel sorry for themselves. Homework doesn't have to cause the grouchies. When you ask your child to clean her room she doesn't have to put on the stubborn mule act. You can control your attitude just as surely as you can control your behavior. You can make a conscious decision to be happy.

Decisions Regarding Thinking

People dig thinking ruts when they let preconceived notions determine their thoughts. You may have a stereotype for different ethnic groups or races. Preconceived notions about certain ethnic groups are a type of thinking rut.

One preconceived notion says that work has to be difficult and play, pleasurable. Trends in fashion can also contribute to thinking ruts: the notion that long hair is liberal and short hair, conservative indicates a preconceived notion.

Another thinking rut says that salesmen exploit the buyer with a "buy to help me" concept. However, many salesmen may be resourceful, i.e., "let me meet your needs." Door-to-door salesmen may annoy you but that does not mean you cannot support your daughter just because the person she wants to marry is a door-to-door salesman.

If you succumb to thinking ruts you let the rut make the decision for you. Thinking ruts become excuses for not thinking responsibly. If your son asks for a dirt bike and your thinking rut says, "Hell's Angels ride motorcycles, therefore all motorcyclists are hell-raisers," you may want to think twice before you tell him he cannot buy a dirt bike. Clear your mind so you can make the decision for yourself rather than letting a thinking rut deny you an independent decision.

People in thinking ruts are like leaves on the water. They go with the flow. They let the current make decisions for them. People in thinking ruts say, "If that clerk's snippy, I'll never shop there again." They let the clerk determine where they shop rather than controlling their own thoughts. If they leave the store without taking the item they came to purchase, who are they punishing? Those who don't want the responsibility of making their own decisions fall into thinking ruts.

Some thinking ruts have labels. "Martyrs" fall into one type of thinking rut. In an effort to end conflict a martyr says, "It's all my fault, I'll take the blame." Rather than resolving the issue at hand, he falls into the habit of "feigned benevolence." Martyrs have discovered that by taking the blame they can end a conflict, so rather than think problems through and come up with the best answer they take the blame themselves.

"Blamers" fall into the opposite thinking rut: "It's not my fault; it's your fault." Rather than staying in a rut, blamers should resolve the issue that is causing conflict. A rut provides a safe place to hide for those who don't want to make their own decisions. They let the tide make it for them.

Ellen fell into a thinking rut called, "If everyone else does it, it must be okay." When Ellen and her friends started to experiment with drugs, Ellen's grades began to drop rapidly. Then she became irritable, prompting her parents to bring her to my office. In addition to resolving to discontinue using drugs, Ellen learned to make thoughtful decisions. She thought before she joined "everybody's doing it" groups. She decided to thoughtfully consider all she heard from her peers and parents before adopting either of their thoughts, on any matter.

Decisions Based on Feelings

Of the three types of decisions that are based on thought (attitudes, thinking, and feeling), decisions based on feelings occur most often. These feelings affect your behavior. If you feel angry you might yell; happy, you might sing; lonely, you might cry.

Decisions based on feelings are more contagious than any other of the nonbehavioral decisions. A smile begets smiles; one rude comment will spread until everybody is in a bad mood. Listen to your friends talk. "I don't want any dessert tonight. I feel like going to bed early." "I want to go skiing tomorrow." "I feel like taking the weekend off." "I want to buy a new Toyota," they say. What people want and what they feel heavily influence their decision-making process.

Terry came home and found his mother banging pots and pans around, muttering under her breath, and slamming cupboards in the kitchen. He decided to get a drink from the bathroom rather than the kitchen.

Another day, he came home to hear his mother singing a chorus out of an opera, and he knew she felt pretty good. So he went to give her a hug and a kiss. Terry didn't weigh any more or stand any taller, but his mother's mood made him feel like a bigger person.

Terry's mother's feelings affected her behavior. Therefore, she wanted to share a kiss when she felt good. Her feelings affected Terry's feelings. Those who learn to control their feelings, regardless of others' behavior, can improve their lives as well as others' lives.

You make many decisions based on your feelings. You get up on Saturday morning and pull out a dresser drawer and say: (a) "Yuck, this drawer needs cleaning out," or (b) "I feel like cleaning this drawer out." When will you most likely clean the drawer? When you say "yuck," or when you feel like cleaning the drawer? Most people clean out drawers, attics, basements, and garages when they feel like it.

Mind Influences Behavior

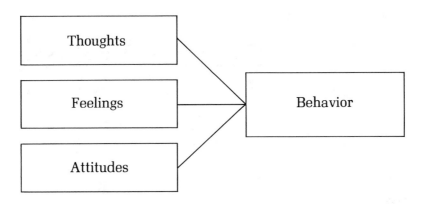

There aren't many people who can leave their garage doors open all day, any day—the garage is just not as clean as the living room. People who clean their attics, basements, and garages when it's necessary, not just when they "feel like it," have learned to control their feelings.

A relationship exists between these four types of decisions: thoughts, feelings, and attitudes influence decisions regarding behavior. Children who learn to consciously control their thoughts, feelings, and attitudes will better control their behavior.

Previously in this book I have discussed different ways children learn to govern their own behavior. The remainder of the book will be devoted to helping children govern their feelings and attitudes.

11

Sensitive Feelings

Don't be so sensitive," you advise your children when they cry over little things. Yet when your spouse brings home flowers to cheer you up on a bad day you may say gratefully, "Thank you for being so sensitive to my needs."

You don't want your children to be so sensitive that they become easily offended, yet you probably want them to be sensitive in the compassionate, empathetic sense. It is wonderful for children to appreciate tenderness and be moved by beautiful things.

This single word, *sensitive*, pigeonholes a variety of emotional responses, some desirable and some not so desirable.

Sensitivity of the Heart

I call the first type of sensitivity, "sensitivity of the heart." For thousands of years the heart has been a symbol for feelings. Phrases such as "being kindhearted," or "goodhearted," or "take heart," illustrate heartfelt feelings.

According to the book of Genesis, Pharaoh hardened his heart and would not let the Israelites out of bondage. The heart is a very ancient symbol for feelings. A heart stands for love, compassion, and understanding.

Sensitivity of the Skin

The heart symbolizes the opposite feeling when someone is referred to as being "hard-hearted." If someone does not seem to have any empathy or understanding for anybody you may think him as hard-hearted or "calloused."

Callouses do not grow on hearts; callouses grown on skin. Skin is a more recent metaphor for feelings. The metaphor for skin and feelings first appeared around Shakespeare's time; for example: "Aah, there's the rub." Phrases such as "letting things get under your skin," "being thin-skinned," "being rubbed the wrong way," "being touchy" refer to the skin.

Skin, a second metaphor for feelings, describes what I call "sensitivity of the skin."

Once you recognize the two types of sensitivity—sensitivity of the heart and sensitivity of the skin—you can help your children avoid negative feelings by getting rid of "thin skin." They can keep the love and affection and compassion for others, but they do not need to allow themselves to be hurt.

Children don't need to give other people the opportunity to make them feel bad. Others' actions need not control how they feel. Even if the offender does not change, your children can avoid letting that individual hurt them.

Three Rules of Dealing with Negative Feelings

Three rules help children avoid hurt feelings:

1. "I am in charge of my mind."
2. "I will not take things personally."

3. "I will try to help the other person." The third rule comes with a corollary: If I cannot help, I will not worry about it.

The following story will illustrate the three rules of dealing with negative feelings.

I Am in Charge of My Mind

Think of yourself at a movie. You come out of the movie and see a drunk leaning against a lamp post. As you watch, three people pass by. A private and his wife pass by, a lieutenant and his wife pass by, and a general and his wife pass by. As they walk by, the drunk screams obscenities at them. (These characters are used for purposes of this specific example and not as reflections of group or class traits.)

The private goes over and punches the drunk in the nose. The lieutenant gets hot under the collar and his ulcers start to bother him, but he keeps walking. The general appears to be deaf. It seems as if he did not hear a thing; he is not even distracted. A few moments later a policeman drives up and says, "I just got a call from the general. A man over here needs my help."

Some people always seem to make situations worse. When it's been a bad day, they pile on the problems. If the vacuum does not work, they may kick it until it really breaks. In this analogy they are the "privates" of the world.

The "lieutenants" of the world try to keep peace. They want peace at any price. They keep all kinds of negative feelings inside without finding an appropriate way to get rid of those negative feelings.

The "generals" of the world wear an "emotional raincoat." They do not let many things get under their skin. They recognize that they control their own minds.

According to the first rule of dealing with negative feelings, your child is in charge of his own mind. If he is in charge of his mind he won't say, "You make me so mad; you tick me off; you frustrate me; you upset me." The person who says these things allows other people to control his feelings. They allow someone else to get inside their minds.

I Will Not Take Things Personally

You can teach your children the second rule for dealing with negative feelings when they are young. The second rule says not to take things personally.

If the little four-year-old next door comes up to you and says, "Those boys down the street are teasing me; they are calling me names," what should you tell him? Should you tell him to go down the street and beat the kids up? That would be hard to do if he is four and they are seven. And you do not want to teach him how to act like the private in the example above.

Should you say, "Come on in the house, dear, and hide under the bed?" That would validate his vulnerability. That would teach him that he is supposed to be upset when people call him names. Instead, teach him, "Sticks and stones may break your bones, but names will never hurt you." Tell him to ignore the other people; he doesn't have to let them make him mad. Tell him not to pay any attention to them. As a matter of fact, if he paid no attention, those who call him names would not be rewarded with control of him and would probably give up.

I Will Try to Help

To help other people, think of their problems. For example, assume that you are taking your daughter on a trip to town to get a gift for her grandmother. In the china department she sees a table laden with beautiful crystal vases. A sign reads, "On sale for $15, regularly $30." One of the vases appears to have gotten into the group by accident; it alone is far more beautiful than all the rest.

Your daughter walks over, picks it up to give it to the sales clerk, and just as she hands it to the sales clerk it gets knocked out of her hand. It smashes into a million pieces. Another sign says, "You break it, you buy it." How does she feel?

The modern psychology magazines say, "If you have it on your chest, get it off," so she turns to share her choice feelings with the Cub Scouts who have been playing tag in the store, but instead of Cub Scouts she sees a little old lady with a white cane and dark glasses.

Will your daughter take the lady's cane and beat her with it? Of course not. She will recognize that the woman's blindness is of much greater significance than a little vase. She forgets her negative feelings and no longer thinks of herself, the vase, or her fifteen bucks. She thinks of the other person. She thinks of how she can help and what she can do for another.

Reinhold Neibur poetically summarized the third rule of dealing with negative feelings in a prayer he once wrote that has since been adopted as the motto of Alcoholics Anonymous: "O God, give us serenity to accept what cannot be changed, courage to change what should be changed, and wisdom to distinguish the one from the other."

Your children will be less vulnerable to negative feelings when they recognize there are things they cannot change and there is no point in worrying about them. They will receive positive feelings when they do something about the things they can change.

Castles

Pretend your children live in a castle, with a courtyard, a moat, and a forest of trees surrounding the castle. Out in the trees, archers shoot bad words and bad deeds at them. One thing I can promise you about life is that there are a lot of archers and they shoot a lot of arrows. If your children take all these arrows personally and sit in a castle with the windows open, the world will make pin cushions out of them.

How do your children protect themselves from the archer's arrows? You could teach them to board up the castle and hide away, protected from the world. But the healthy solution is to be aware of the world and try to help the archers. When the arrows start to fly, close the castle windows.

To close castle windows and not allow the archers to hurt your child, teach your child the three rules of dealing with negative feelings. If he is tempted to say, "You make me so mad," he can stop and realize who is in charge of his mind. He does not want to keep his castle windows open and allow the arrows inside. He does not want to let the people in the woods take control of his mind.

When your four-year-old neighbor complains about name-calling you can teach him to ignore the arrows. He need not take their rudeness personally so that it disrupts his life.

When people shoot arrows from as near as the castle walls, children can follow the same rule. Siblings sit on the wall and are closer to one another than the archers in the woods. Brothers and sisters often shoot arrows from across the room and always seem to shoot the sharpest arrows at those they love.

Children learn to ignore those arrows when you teach them that out in the woods are many blind ladies. Many people do not see that they are shooting arrows. The people do not see where those arrows are going. They do not see that their arrows actually hit their loved ones. Out in the woods there are those with handicaps and problems who may literally be blind, stupid, dumb, illiterate, immature, or childish, even hostile and attacking.

Whatever their problem is, it's their problem. The principles used to cope with the arrows are still the same: (1) I am

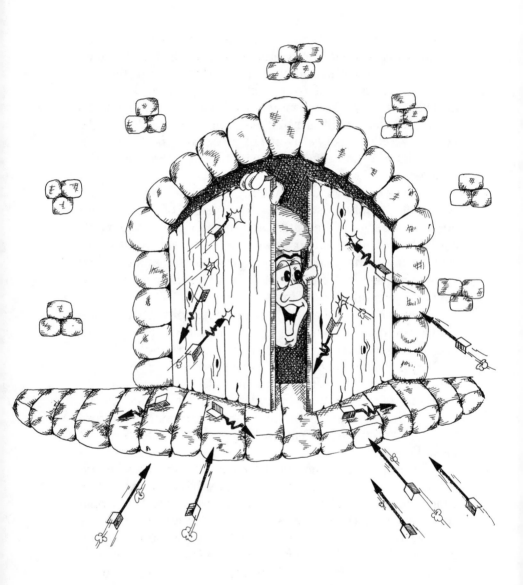

Castle Windows

in charge of my mind. (2) I will not take the behavior of others personally. (3) I will try to help the other person if I can. If not, I will ignore them.

The child who has mastered these principles might say, "You don't make me mad. You don't make me sad. You don't even make me happy. You don't *make* me anything. I will be happy whether or not I'm invited to your birthday party."

If a boy sends roses to your daughter and she's allergic to roses, they won't come in the castle. But if she's not allergic she'll put them on the piano and say, "Thank you so much, the roses are beautiful." This child can *let* others make her happy, but she's still in charge of her own feelings, even feelings of happiness.

The archers in the woods often have problems greater than your own, and if your child can be aware of their ignorance, she can make sure they do not influence how she behaves.

Ignoring Versus Exploiting

When your children master the three rules of dealing with negative feelings they may encounter another challenge.

A sixth-grade girl came into my office with this story: "Last Friday my teacher gave a midyear social studies test," she said. "I knew I could do well on the test because I had studied all year long. During the test I noticed the boy in the seat next to me copying my answers. It wasn't really fair, because he didn't deserve a good grade. But I didn't want to get him in trouble. I wanted to be a nice friend and I wanted him to like me."

What if that little boy had wanted to rob a bank? Would she have driven his getaway car? Who is the little girl concerned about really? Many people pretend that they are thinking of others when actually they are avoiding the responsibility of protecting their own castle. They allow others to take advantage of them.

When I suggest that your children ignore the archers from the woods, I am not suggesting that if someone crosses over the wall, comes in the castle, marches in the front hall, breaks up the furniture, and starts a fire, the children ignore the intruder. Sticks and stones may bounce off walls, but bombs and tear gas really hurt.

Children who respond to archers in an effective, definite manner can protect their own stewardship and also deter the archers who want to practice their archery.

It does not benefit the other person to allow him to practice thievery. For the attacker's benefit let him know, "Here is the castle wall; do not cross it." Within their own stewardship people can do what they want to, but when they come into your child's stewardship, they are to behave according to her rules. Your child can be in charge of her mind and not allow others to upset her, and at the same time prevent others from coming into her stewardship and destroying it.

12

Wedges in the Window

The same sharp arrow may come again and again until your child cannot seem to ignore it. It is more difficult for her to close her windows when the archers shoot this particular arrow at her. The arrows may differ for each person, but some arrows are common to everybody and everybody has a difficult time ignoring them.

When your youngsters have difficulty closing their windows to a particular arrow they may have a wedge holding that window open. Such wedges therefore make them vulnerable to hurt.

The Caring Wedge

One of my patients, whom I'll call Melanie, attended Chelwood Elementary School. One day at lunch her friends told her about a girl in another sixth-grade class who was denied a part in the school play. The girl was very talented and looked forward to performing in front of her classmates. However, she had asthma and the teachers didn't want to concern themselves with a possible attack during rehearsals or at the play, so they would not cast her in the play.

"Isn't it awful about the play?" Melanie's friend said.

"Yeah, it's awful," she replied.

"But it's just terrible."

"Yeah, it's terrible."

"Doesn't it just upset you?"

"No, no," Melanie said. "I was listening to Dr. Goates a while back and I decided to shut my windows."

"Shut what?"

"Yeah, I'm not going to let things get to me; I'm not going to take things personally. If I can change things fine, but otherwise I won't worry about it."

Then Melanie's friend looked at her and said, "Don't you care?"

The wedge that keeps many windows open says, "You are supposed to get upset to prove you care."

I actually had a young girl come into my office one day after her mother's funeral. "I'm very concerned," she said. "I cried my eyes out for three days after Mother died, but when I went to the funeral there were no tears."

I asked her, "So why are you coming into my office?"

"Doctor, what will people think?" she questioned in response.

Her concern about what other people would think had left her vulnerable. She left her castle windows open. She knew she was grieving over the loss of her mother, but she was vulnerable to people who thought she should act upset to prove she cared.

If your son were playing on a football team and one of the players got hit particularly hard, he could show his concern without jumping around and screaming, "Blood, blood, blood! The bone in the arm's showing!"

It is far more important to be in charge of his castle and be effective than it is to prove how much he cares by getting upset. Getting upset really does not help anybody. In fact getting upset is contagious and is likely to upset only more people. I like the expression, "You lose your cool, you lose."

A Wedge Called State-Dependent Learning

Your children have possibly told you, "I'll never raise my kids the way you are raising me." Yet when they have children they will sound just like their parents; state-dependent learning (learning that occurs only in a specific environment) often causes the environment to dictate behavior.

If you forget someone's name, you can sometimes mentally put yourself in the environment where you first heard the name and it might come to you. If you were introduced in the foyer of the church, you can picture yourself in that setting and often you will remember the name.

In a domestic setting, state-dependent learning causes you or your children to behave the way you learned in your first domicile. Under stress you may find you sound just like your parents did. Likewise, your children may say the same choice words you say, even in the same tone of voice.

At the office you might learn not to let the office interpersonal relationships bother you. You can remove that wedge and close your castle windows and not allow disagreements to cause yelling and screaming. Yet when you come home to a domestic setting, under stress that wedge creeps back in. Disagreements at home are too similar to childhood experiences. You may have learned to respond with yelling and screaming.

At a conscious level you can remove the wedge in this generation. Grease the hinges and shut the windows. Remember the three rules of dealing with negative feelings illustrated by our castle: I'm in charge of my mind. I will not take things personally, at work or at home. I will help when I can and not worry when I can't.

The Manipulation Wedge

Another wedge frequently sticks in a youngster's castle windows and holds the windows open unnecessarily. The following story describes this wedge.

Once upon a time there was a gorgeous valley with beautiful castles. These old castles had stood for a long time. And the people who lived in these castles had all learned how to get along with their neighbors in their castles.

One day a new chap came into the valley and started to build himself a new castle. Out on the front porch he put some signs: "I'll be happy if . . ." and "I'll be mad if you don't . . ." On the back porch there were signs that said: "If you love me you will . . ." and "If you don't, you don't love me."

The neighbors came over to visit this new chap and they saw the signs on the front porch. The signs said, "I'll be happy if . . ." and "I'll be mad if you don't . . ." On the signs were listed all the duties good neighbors can do. So the neighbors began to trim his hedges and paint his fences. They were doing all the good things the signs said that neighbors do to welcome a new castle builder.

As they worked the fellow that built the new castle did not get happy. In fact, he stayed kind of irritable. "There are not enough people helping," he said. "They're not working hard enough. They're not doing things right. They're not doing things my way. Nothing is ever good enough."

What will these neighbors in the other castles do with this new neighbor that has come into the neighborhood? Soon they will have their barbecues without him. It will not take long before they decide to ignore him. "See, I told you this was a crummy neighborhood," he will say.

Now, why doesn't that chap take his signs down and join the barbecues? Because if he did, how could he control the neighbors? How would he get his fences painted, and hedges trimmed if he couldn't control people by playing, "I'd be happy if . . ." and "I'll be mad if you don't . . ."? He might have to say please and thank you or even pay teenagers to do the work.

Your children will try to manipulate you. Their friends will try to manipulate them. Some parents try to govern their children through manipulation. I have seen marriages break up over that kind of mutual control. I have seen teenagers run away from homes. And as long as people are willing to paint fences and trim hedges, the signs will remain.

Where did that chap get signs like that? They came with the stork. They hang right over the crib. They say, "I'll be happy if you change my pants, but I'll scream if you don't. I'll be happy if you feed me regularly, and I'll scream if you don't." Infants would like you to believe they are born poor and helpless. (Helpless, my foot.) Infants are in control of the whole family. You will even get up in the middle of the night for an infant that is playing "I'll be happy if . . ."

When a child gets to be about two years old and says, "Mom, give me a drink of milk or I'll have a temper tantrum," the mother says, "It is time we took your signs down. If you'd like a drink of milk you say please. And when you get your milk you say thank you. If I hear any tantrums you'll be scooted to the bedroom, out of the sight of polite company."

"I don't believe that; I've been controlling this family for years," the two-year-old says. So he will try a few temper tantrums. When he ends up in the bedroom he will think, "What's this world coming to—I'm loosing my grip. I can't control everybody anymore." But he will notice his parents still play "I'll be happy if . . ." And he will notice his older brothers and sisters play "I'll be happy if . . ." If he can get away with playing "I'll be happy if . . ." in any relationship, he will. And he will continue to control those who reward him when he plays the game. That is why we sometimes see children and adolescents trying to manipulate and control each other, rather than learning how to say please and thank you and giving honest rewards for honest efforts.

Your child will better govern herself when she can shut those windows so that she is not vulnerable to those who would manipulate and control her. It would be best if she avoided manipulating and controlling others as well.

13

Buckets of
Feelings

How much is a pound of love? Can you measure a yard of anger? You can see the results of feelings —a kiss may be the result of love or a black eye the result of anger. But feelings themselves are too abstract to see, and people understand better the things they can visualize.

A man with many concerns may say, "I feel like I have the weight of the world on my shoulders." He measures his feelings by comparing them to the world.

Twenty years ago I first drew a diagram to help people picture positive and negative feelings. I have been using it ever since then. When people see the diagram, they learn to better understand their feelings.

The diagram depicts two buckets like those the Dutch milkmaids used to carry. A long wooden support rested across the milkmaid's shoulders, and pails dangled from either end. You carry similar buckets that are invisible: in one bucket you hold your positive feelings and in the other bucket you hold your negative feelings.

Buckets of Feelings

A child's feelings influence the way he behaves and the way he makes decisions.

Positive Feelings

The feelings your children get when you say, "Thank you for doing your chores without being asked," fill up the positive bucket. When someone smiles at them or compliments, hugs, or congratulates them, the feelings fill their positive buckets.

You can fill your children's positive buckets by recognizing their achievements. Children overtly ask for recognition. When your little girl draws something at school she will bring it home and say, "See what I did." Little boys create sculptures from rocks and shells and present them in anticipation of approval. They won't destroy the Lego building, the puzzle, the train track, or the sand castle until they show someone who will appreciate their work.

Verbal affection, such as saying "I love you," "I'm proud of you," "You did a good job," "You're a great kid," and "You make our family happy" fill up a positive bucket.

(In chapter 4 I discussed cautions for praising youngsters. As children grow, their buckets get bigger and their capacity to handle a lot of positive feelings increases.)

Physical affection is another way to fill up positive buckets. A professor once told me, "If you get three hugs a day you'll never be blue." If you hug your children and hold them on your lap or walk hand in hand, their positive buckets will be filled. A kiss on a skinned knee works miracles to take away the sting.

Some people's positive buckets overflow. I call people with full positive buckets "my cup runneth over" people. They are full of positive feelings. You enjoy being around these kind of people. When you plan a party you want to invite "my cup runneth over" people. In fact, all you have to do to have a fun party is invite those kind of people, provide food, and they will entertain themselves.

You enjoy it when these people come around because they act happy. Happy people make you feel good. They have enough joy inside that they can share some with others. If they have any problems, they seem to have them under control and are willing to listen to your problems.

The saying "The rich get richer and the poor get poorer" applies to feelings as well as money. Those with full positive buckets draw more positive feelings. They get invited to parties and they dance in the center of the ballroom because people like to be around them.

If your children give happiness to others, others will give it back. Friends will flock around them, call them on the telephone to talk, comment on how good your child makes them feel. All this positive feedback fills their positive buckets even more. Someone once said, "Happiness is like perfume, you can't spray it on others without getting a little on yourself."

Negative Feelings

When castle windows are left open your children may experience disappointment, frustration, anger; they may become upset or feel bad. These feelings go in the negative bucket. When someone yells at them and the arrows fly, the feelings go in the negative bucket. When your children criticize themselves or dwell on their failures, they fill up their own negative buckets.

Some people's negative buckets overflow. They have negative feelings to spill on others. If you visit a person with too many negative feelings and try to tell them about a tragedy, they will recite their whole library of grievances to you before they will listen to someone else's troubles.

I saw an old woman do this when she went to visit her niece who was dying of cancer. The old woman sat in a chair by the hospital bed and described how the niece's grandmother had died of the same type of cancer: "Died a horrible death, she did."

Dale Carnegie taught that the best way to make friends is to "talk in terms of the other man's interests." So when a negative person pours out his overwhelming grievances, no one cares anyway. Negative people actually drive away would-be friends.

Just as positive people attract positive feelings, negative people attract negative feelings. Unfortunately, negativism has a boomerang effect. Your children probably don't like to be around a negative friend so they avoid the friend, which makes him feel even worse about himself because he is ostracized. If someone has the reputation of being "boring," only the rare individual makes the effort to find out it's not true.

People with full negative buckets are unhappy people. They have so many extra negative feelings spilling out of their buckets that they're desperate to give some away to others. No wonder no one wants to associate with them.

An unfortunate imbalance in buckets exists. Someone once said it takes five smiles to erase one frown. This rule applies particularly to adolescents. Your teenagers are so self-conscious anyway that one drop in the negative bucket far outweighs a positive one. If your daughter wore a new dress to school and another child laughed at how it looked, it would take five people to tell her how nice she looked before she could forget the insult.

For this reason, parents must take special care to fill a child's positive bucket. Though each child differs, as discussed in chapter 5, you will want to criticize less frequently than you praise, because negative buckets tend to fill up so fast anyway.

Buckets of Varying Size

Buckets come large and they come small. The expression "He's a big person" means he's big in psychological stature;

117

he handles problems well. Big people can deal graciously with a lot of feelings. A "big" person has big buckets.

Big people develop a great capacity to deal with the problems of life. They can hold a lot of negative feelings without spilling some on others. They can also hold a lot of positive feelings and become positive people.

The homecoming queen at Central High School was a big person. Karen had thick blonde hair that extended past her waist. Her tan face accented her hazel eyes and gleaming white teeth. The most exclusive department store in town invited Karen to model for them. She earned straight A's in school and tutored other students in math.

The "girl with everything" attracted people to her like flowers do bees. Karen liked everyone and treated everyone as if they were important. Though potential rivals, Karen's girlfriends never felt jealous of her. Everyone wanted to be her friend. She made them feel important and treated them as nice as anyone could.

Karen dealt graciously with all the positive feelings put into her bucket and she did not become arrogant or embarrassed. Although she didn't spill it all over, Karen's negative bucket was full too. Her father was having an affair and her mother wanted a divorce. Her brother, with three children, had lost his job. Karen could find ample reason to complain and spill negative feelings. Instead, she had learned to draw more positive feelings.

Life Stretches Buckets

Life enlarges a child's capacity to deal with problems. The experiences of life stretch your buckets. The more adversity children encounter and handle successfully, the more aptly they will deal with adversity.

The opposite of a big person would of course be a little person. Petty jealousies, complaints, and insignificant irritants annoy little people.

Children are people who have not encountered a great deal of adversity nor an abundance of joy. They need to grow and experience life to help them develop the ability to deal with feelings appropriately.

Toddlers playing in the sandbox usually have little buckets. If one toddler swipes the sandpail, the other toddler immediately goes crying to Mommy. Toddlers have not learned to hold a lot of negative feelings without spilling them on others.

Experience, not age, enlarges buckets. An overprotected child will grow into an adult who cannot deal graciously with feelings. He might deal with problems artificially by anesthetizing the pain with alcohol or drugs. This arrests an individual's ability to learn how to handle life's challenges. A child who experiences fame or a great deal of adversity may develop a large capacity to deal with feelings. This ability makes them mature beyond their years.

Lids on Buckets

Sometimes people put lids on their buckets. People who are bereft of praise (chapter 3) have lids on their buckets. They do not allow feelings in the positive bucket, nor do they drain feelings from their negative bucket.

A big person learns to accept compliments and attention as graciously as they accept criticism and anger. Children need to allow others to fill their positive buckets and express thanks when they receive gifts or praise. It's all right to acknowledge a well-deserved compliment.

You probably know people who will not allow you to give them compliments. You say something nice and they try to turn it around.

"You sang beautifully," you say.

"Oh, no, I sounded breathy and flat."

Other people will not even acknowledge compliments.

"Your hair looks lovely," you say.

"Well, it's the only thing that worked."

As discussed in chapter 4, such behavior causes an individual to become bereft of praise.

How much more appropriate to respond, "Thank you. You are so kind to notice."

Holding negative feelings in too long will cause an explosion. Those with too many negative feelings inside often develop physical signs such as asthma, ulcers, colitis, migraines, or skin diseases. Children may become withdrawn, refuse to eat, wet the bed, or become horrid and unmanageable. The importance of draining your negative bucket is evident.

Marcie, the wife of a psychiatric resident I knew, spent a week in the hospital because her negative feelings began to eat away at her. Marcie's husband would come home from work every day and tell his wife about the patients he had seen. In a very pleasant and conversational way he expressed his concerns and thus emptied his negative bucket. Marcie, in turn, began to feel so awful about these people that her negative feelings built up inside. She lay awake worrying while he slept. She didn't want to burden her husband, but instead she developed a skin rash. She began scratching until she damaged her skin to the point that she required hospitalization.

Some people have funnels on their negative buckets. They collect grief. They read the obituaries before they read the comics. When I lived in Europe, I observed women who habitually attended funerals. I called them "funeral aunts." They came to funerals just to cry and mourn even though they were totally unacquainted with the deceased. They wanted to spend their dying days wallowing in grief.

The opposite extreme from children who spill negative buckets all over others are those who become emotionally plugged up. The next chapter describes how to express feelings in a healthy way. You can teach your children to express their feelings appropriately so that you need never combat temper tantrums. Children can also develop a large positive bucket, full of good feelings that they can share with others.

Your objective as parents is to help your children learn how to fill their positive buckets and how to tactfully empty a negative bucket. Everyone needs a "smorgasbord" of good feelings coming into their positive buckets and a dumping ground to get rid of negative feelings.

14

Time, Place,
Method

The family resembles a corporation in a number of ways. The management team in a corporation must meet often; also the managers of the home must meet often. The family deals with personnel, assets, liabilities, cash flow, accounts receivable, accounts payable, health benefits, and employee relations—just like a corporation.

"Corporate officers" in a family need to get together and discuss the dynamics of their program and their goals. As the primary product in the home is healthy personnel, parents must care for the family's emotional needs as carefully as the physical needs or any other needs in the family.

You and your spouse, the corporate officers, might want to take a long drive together to find some time for a management meeting. Every eight weeks or so you might even take a weekend vacation retreat to discuss the dynamics of your family organization without phone calls or children interrupting. At these major management meetings you can clean out negative buckets; discuss the size of your child's pen; discuss whether consequences are working; and review the family's relationships.

Weekend getaways, though nice for management meetings, are too infrequent. Negative feelings may not wait, so if you or your child wants to express negative feelings you may want to call a special management meeting. The purpose of calling a specific meeting is that it assures you choose the proper *time* to empty negative buckets.

Time

The proper time to discuss negative feelings is when you are not hurried or rushed. Choose a time when you do not have so much on your mind that you can't concentrate on your feelings or on your children's feelings. Right before you walk out of the house on your way to work is not the time for a family management meeting.

You will not want to clean out a negative bucket just before bed. It may ruin the night's sleep. Start early when you are not tired and you have time to resolve problems without destroying your peaceful sleep time.

Before dinner may not be the best time to clean out negative buckets either. It may ruin dinner. Besides, your children are possibly hungry and impatient.

Each person should agree on the proper time to meet and prepare to discuss their feelings. If your child has asked to have a family management meeting about how you give unfair privileges, you need time to think about your discussion. You may decide he is right and the meeting will be over as soon as you agree to be more fair. You may need time to think about how to explain to your child what is "fair" about your ways.

If your child suddenly shouted, "You're not fair," and expressed negative feelings without choosing an appropriate time, you may react at the spur of the moment. You may shout back, "Don't bug me; you do what I say because I'm your father." Then feelings don't get resolved, just dumped from one person's bucket into another person's bucket, often with added malice.

Children find it particularly difficult to wait for the right time to empty their negative buckets. They have little patience, and with their castle windows open they anger easily. Your toddler probably screams the instant his friend takes the toy he wanted to play with. As your toddler grows older will he allow his friends to take the toy. He will eventually learn to discuss the matter with his friends, "The Battlestar is mine. You bring your own spaceship next time."

Place

The neighbor children in the sandbox do not want to hear you empty your negative bucket. If your children just tracked sand all over the house, call them aside to share your negative feelings about their behavior. Do not yell in front of their friends in the sandbox.

Select the proper *place* to hold a management meeting. Your two-year-old may throw a temper tantrum in the grocery store because you won't buy her Twinkies. But you know it's not best to indulge her and buy the Twinkies. Spanking a screaming child in the middle of the store will not solve the dispute. It is appropriate to leave your full grocery cart in the aisle and take your child to the car, where she can express her negative feelings and where you can discuss the proper way to ask for Twinkies.

Method

The proper *method* of emptying a negative bucket is as important as the proper time and place. When you take your finger and point it at somebody's chest and start pounding on their bare breastbone, it does not take very many taps before it begins to hurt. One good method to express negative feelings is the "I message."

Do not say, "You numbskull, you knucklehead, you ate all the chocolate chips I was saving for cookies. You know you're supposed to stay out of the cupboards. You make me so mad; you, you . . ." It does not take very many "taps on the bare breastbone" before you develop a defensive relationship. The person who ate the chocolate will want to defend himself.

The "I messages" that Thomas Gordon teaches provide an effective method of expressing feelings. "I messages" encourage you to tap your own breastbone rather than someone else's. When the chips are gone you might say, "I could not find any chocolate chips this morning. I had really wanted to make some cookies today. I guess I allowed myself to become pretty disappointed when they disappeared."

If you can point your finger at yourself to express your feelings rather than at somebody else, you can prevent a defensive response. When you point your finger at yourself, whoever ate the chocolate may develop negative feelings. They may feel a little bit of remorse or a little bit of guilt, but they will also want to make up for their mistake.

When you point a finger at yourself rather than the other person, his response becomes positive. He may say, "Well, Mom, what do you want me to do about it? Do you want me to run to the store and buy some more? I'm sorry that I ate the chips; I won't do it again." An apology and repairing the mistake sure beats an argument between two defensive people.

You can use the "I method" when expressing negative feelings to your children: "Timmy, I was so disappointed when you left your bicycle in the middle of the driveway. I thought you were old enough to remember to put it away. I feel bad that it got run over."

Those who express negative feelings will also want to control the tone of voice and volume with which they speak. When you point a finger at yourself it is easier not to use the harsh words or hard hand you might when pointing at someone else. When you express negative feelings without yelling, no one will be tempted to yell back.

The same method you would use to criticize yourself will work when you criticize others. (Remember the old "do unto others" rule?) Express your negative feelings in a soft voice; control the anger you feel so the person you are angry with will feel free to respond. When someone is chasing you with a whip you are not likely to stop and say, "Let's discuss this." Likewise, your child will not want to stay around and fight when they know the atmosphere is not conducive to discussion.

Sometimes the best method for expressing negative feelings is on paper. When your teenager has time to read your negative feelings he can think about them and "cool down" before responding.

People who express negative feelings would benefit if they were willing to accept another view. Listen to the person you are talking to and agree to change if his suggestion helps. If Billy has negative feelings because the coach only put him in for two innings of the softball game he might well listen when Mother explains that with twenty-two players, a compromise must be reached. It will do Billy more good to listen to Mother than to spill his negative bucket on her.

I call the right time, place, and method the "TPM." Remind your children to wait for the right TPM when they start to express negative feelings in an inappropriate manner. You can also remind yourself how to express disappointment in this way.

When you find the right TPM, it allows both parties to appropriately let the other person know how you feel. Only after they understand your feelings can they deal with them.

Children who express negative feelings inappropriately will not get rid of their negative feelings. All screaming does is cause more negative feelings in the person who hears the complaint and in the one who makes it. With the proper TPM, children can learn to empty their negative buckets when, where, and in a manner that will encourage others to listen.

15

Emptying Buckets

Children seem to find many occasions to vent their negative feelings. They use their parents as resources and say, "Mama, he hit me. He took my sweater. I can't find my socks." This happens in everybody's house. The children have small buckets and they have not learned to handle the little problems in life. They get their feelings out immediately.

Parents have relatively empty negative buckets, so they can deal with the negative feelings of the children. As the children get rid of their negative feelings, the parents dry their tears and pat them on the back and say, "There, there, you are going to be all right." Parents give their children comfort. This is a nice system in which to rear children.

When your children begin getting feelings "off their chest," that relieves their burden. As you recognize their relief you might find joy in helping them feel better. You will probably take parental satisfaction in being a resource to your children. You will feel good about helping them, and this joy actually fills your own positive bucket.

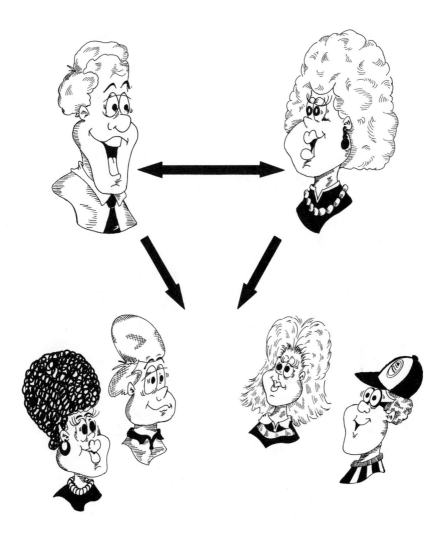

Resource Chain

I have put the children in the resource diagram in a straight line. This is not necessarily realistic. Older children can also be a resource to younger children. But that is usually an apprenticeship, an opportunity the children have to learn to be a resource. The primary responsibility for rearing the children still rests with the parents because they are the ones who are concerned with the childrens' emotional needs.

A Resource for Mom and Dad

Parents are for the benefit of children, not children for the benefit of parents. That may sound obvious, but when you think about it, it is a relatively new idea.

Fathers used to raise their daughters in hopes they could negotiate a nice dowry as if the girl were one of the cattle. Farmers used to raise sons so they could till the farm, and if they had six hundred acres of land and no sons, they would not have any money in the bank. Somebody had to run that farm. One hundred years ago, children were a financial asset.

Today, in most circumstances, children are a financial liability. In fact, the statistics say it will cost over one hundred thousand dollars to rear a child and send him to college. Such challenges can seem overwhelming to parents. So what happens when you, as a parent, need a resource?

Sometimes Mom and Dad need someone to pat them on their backs and fill their positive buckets just like the children do. You remember the lady I mentioned who would sit near the hospital bed of her niece dying of cancer and talk about all the horrible diseases she had known?

When you need a resource you will want to pick somebody who has a relatively empty negative bucket. In addition, this person might take some satisfaction in helping you feel better, just as you help your children.

This individual you find to share your burden may at times come to you and say, "Last week you were getting feelings off your chest and I patted you on the back; could I spend a few minutes with you and tell you about my problems?" Your resource, then, takes a turn to get feelings off his back. When two people spend time together and get feelings off their chests or pat each other on the back, that becomes an important part of friendship.

If your friend lives in Los Angeles and you live in New York, you may run up a big phone bill. It is a lot nicer if you have a friend that lives close to you. It would really be nice to have a friend under the same roof. And the nicest thing of all would be if your friend were your spouse.

After a couple has been married for a while they learn how to exchange feelings, get things off their chests, encourage each other, and pat each other on the back. They get closer to one another. The expression "They are very close" often means the couple are a resource to one another. After this close couple has been married for fifty years they can stand up in front of their progeny and say, "We never had a cross word in our lives." (Of course, they are getting senile and they can't remember.)

Short Circuits

Unfortunately, this resource system does not exist in many families. For example, 24 percent of all households have no father. Who is going to miss the father in this system? The children may miss Daddy, but the children still have some resource in Mother. But who is Mother's resource? Who is helping clean out her negative bucket, and who is helping pat her on the back?

If you attempt to call a mother with no husband and the phone is always busy, she is probably desperately trying to get some relationships going to meet her emotional needs. In this household without a father, the children often have an underresourced mother.

I also find households where one parent does not care. I

know more than one father who says, "Lady, I promised you food, clothes, and shelter, but I never promised to be your friend." In such households the father is frequently parked outside a club and the mother is domestically overburdened and underresourced. Mother's role is to be confined to the house with all its duties and to deal with the children, without a father's assistance.

Other households exist where the father or mother cares but does not help. This type of parent comes home from work, gets out of the car in the rain, in front of the garage door with the automatic lift. He moves the bicycles to get the car into the garage, then goes in the house and yells at his spouse because dinner is not ready; the spouse then yells at the oldest child because she has not set the table; she yells at the next child because he did not help; and finally, the little guy goes out and beats up the cat. Everybody in this type of family just passes negative feelings around. They don't learn how to resolve negative feelings and to be resources to one another.

The optimal household has a mother who can assess the father's temperament, and a father who comes home and checks out the mother's apron strings. He evaluates the situation to see how Mother is feeling. If the apron bow is tied on one side it has been a good day and if on the other side it has been a bad day. If it has been a good day this father may sit down and talk to his wife about his negative bucket. If it has been a bad day he may show the kids out of the kitchen and listen to her. These two individuals can then meet each others' needs. The father might then help with the dinner dishes, put the children to bed, and read the newspaper. Then Mother may say, "Dear, have you got some time that we could talk, a week from Thursday, around noon?" This couple knows how to be resources to one another. The management team of this household takes some time to be together.

Those who live in households that do not run in the traditional manner need not despair. If only one parent lives in the home, if the other parent does not care, or if the other parent cares but does not help, you can still provide a resource to your children. It may require that a single parent learn to find his or her own resource. It may require that the two parents learn to be resources to one another. The object is to help your children find an appropriate resource that they can utilize when they need to express negative feelings.

16

Realistic
Goals

Picture a two-year-old named Jimmy, playing in the nursery with his friend. His mother has a goal for the boys: "Please pick up all the toys," she asks and offers a story as a reward. Then she walks to the kitchen to set the table for lunch.

When she returns to the nursery, what will happen if she anticipates that all those toys will be put away? How will she feel when she opens the door to the nursery?

Jimmy will not have picked up those toys. When left alone he will probably have made an even bigger mess. The reality is that few two-year-olds are able to pick up toys when left alone.

Neither can an eight-year-old do dishes as well as an adult. She might forget to wipe the counters and sweep the floor, or her mom may find a little food stuck to the large pots. The disparity between Mother's image of a spotless kitchen (your anticipations) and a half-clean kitchen (reality) creates many negative feelings.

The distance between your anticipations and reality determines the degree of your negative feelings. You will

Anticipations Disparity

100%	Large disparity = Many negative feelings		100%	Perfection is still the goal, but the individual does not depend on attaining it to be happy.
				No disparity = No negative feelings
	50%		50%	50%
Anticipations	Reality		Anticipations	Reality

experience greater negative feelings if your children don't even come close to behaving as you want them to than if they fall only a little short of your anticipated goal.

Emotional Dependence

It is possible to avoid negative feelings when you learn not to be emotionally dependent on the goal you set for yourself or your children. Pursue goals with the thought "If this fails, I won't fret" rather than "If this fails, I'll just die."

I know a man who actually did die when reality differed from his anticipated goal. Most people who knew Moroni Jensen agree he "died of a broken heart." Jensen was running for lieutenant governor in my state several years ago. (At that time the lieutenant governor ran independent of the governor.)

Just before the final election the gubernatorial candidate was found to be behind in the polls and was in jeopardy of losing the election. Jensen's party pulled the funds they had promised him for television advertising and gave them to the man who was running for governor.

The party won the gubernatorial race while Jensen, the candidate for lieutenant governor, lost. Three days later Jensen died suddenly of heart failure. He was devastated because his anticipations of party support were so different from the reality of the withdrawn funds.

People who become emotionally dependent on a goal (leave their castle windows open) become vulnerable to events and people they cannot control. If you do not become emotionally dependent on your goals, you will not become disappointed, frustrated, or upset if you cannot reach those goals.

Reality

To avoid negative feelings, reduce your anticipations. Joseph B. Wirthlin once joked, "I didn't expect much so I was rarely disappointed." His observation is actually quite insightful, though probably said in jest.

Reality includes your child's age limitations, external temptations, emotional maturity, and motor skills. Perhaps two-year-olds can't clean up the nursery because they can't concentrate on one task long enough. They may not be strong enough to push the rocking horse into the corner. Their coordination might fail when wrapping kite string around a stick. Most eight-year-olds don't clean a kitchen perfectly because either they haven't had the experience to know that clean floors and counters constitute a clean kitchen or they lack the discipline to follow through on a task.

Children may be physically capable of a task yet may find their self-discipline is underdeveloped. Physically, toddlers can stay out of the cookie jar but most can't control their desires. Sometimes even older children can't control their desire to watch television when they need to do homework.

If your eight-year-old daughter wanted to do a good job of cleaning the kitchen, but her girlfriend came over and wanted her to leave before she started on the floor and the counters, she might not be mature enough to tell her girlfriend, "No, please wait." External factors may be too tempting to the little girl.

Even an adolescent's ability to reach certain goals fluctuates from day to day. A typical adolescent will be obedient one day and rebellious the next. Adolescents learn consistent responsibility gradually. They seem to progress five steps forward and four steps back.

Jim, a fourteen-year-old Boy Scout, caused endless problems at home. He lied to his parents and once the police caught him shoplifting. Yet Jim was capable of good behavior too. Once his Scout troop needed new Scout uniforms. The uniforms were paid for, but the Scoutmaster hadn't found time to go pick them up yet. Jim hopped on his bike and rode to the Scout office. He picked up the shirts with the patches and rode home. Then he sewed all nine patches to the shirts for his Scoutmaster.

Jim then reverted to bad behavior, forgetting his curfew, but later demonstrated responsibility by mowing a widow's lawn without being asked.

It does not matter that your child *should* reach his goals. Your daughter *should* be stronger than her friend. Children *should* be self-disciplined enough to ignore the television or the cookie jar. Regardless of what your children should be capable of, parents must recognize what they are capable of.

To avoid getting angry, remember that the child in the nursery is only two years old. Refrain from forming such high anticipations of him. When you go down to the nursery, say, "Woopee, you put the teddy bear and the dolly away! Now help me put the blocks away."

Adults who recognize the limitations of their children and adolescents can remain happy. You can avoid becoming disappointed if you don't become emotionally dependent on a perfect performance in the first place. Rather than anticipate that the whole kitchen be cleaned up, anticipate that your children do the best they can do.

A Child's Expectations

Year after year children write to Santa to give him their Christmas lists. They underline everything in the Sears and Roebuck catalog and say, "Santa Claus, here's my list. This is what I expect from you." Then they put the list in a stocking and leave two cookies and a glass of milk on the kitchen table. (Even Santa receives a reward for reaching his goals.) If those children go to bed emotionally dependent and anticipating everything on that list, how will they feel Christmas morning?

You will want to help them so they don't ruin Christmas morning with disappointment. To help your children avoid becoming emotionally dependent on that whole list, you might say, "Now, Santa has a lot of children to visit so don't anticipate getting everything on your list." Children may be prepared to have realistic expectations because, in reality, not everything on that list will appear under the Christmas tree.

Still, you don't need to have the children cross off every other item on the list. It is not necessary to say, "Go throw away the bottom half of the list." You can allow your children to maintain the entire list as a goal, while encouraging them not to become dependent on the goal. This way young children learn how to enjoy Christmas regardless of which gifts come.

Jane and Michael Banks learned this lesson in the movie Mary Poppins. They wrote a list of qualifications for a nanny.

If you want this choice position,
have a cheery disposition,
rosy cheeks, no warts, play games, all sorts.
You must be kind you must be witty,
very sweet and fairly pretty.
Take us on outings, give us treats, sings songs,
bring sweets.
Never be cross or cruel,
never give us castor oil or gruel.
Love us as a son or daughter,
and never smell of barley water.
If you won't scold and dominate us,
we will never give you cause to hate us.
We won't hide your spectacles so you can't see,
put toads in your bed or pepper in your tea. . . .

The children expected their nanny to fit all the qualifications. But if she lost her temper on the first day, they wouldn't want to give up on her. Unless they realized, "Well, she's new on the job," they would go through a nanny a week.

Dependence on Perfection

Unfortunately, some of today's adults did not learn as children to separate their Christmas lists from reality. They have become dependent on perfection.

When Daddy works for someone else his paycheck comes regularly every payday. He becomes so dependent on that regular paycheck that he may decide, "Since my paycheck comes Friday, I'm going to go buy my son a new bicycle Thursday night." What happens when Daddy goes to work Friday morning and the personnel department says, "Sorry, the computer's broken. You won't get your check until next Wednesday?" The check Daddy wrote for the bicycle may bounce.

Nine percent of the people in this country are farmers. Of the remaining 91 percent only 9 percent work for themselves. People who work for a company can become dependent on the company.

Farmers' families know better than to depend on anything. In spite of the almanac, no one can predict the weather. If farmers became emotionally dependent on their harvest, they would be disappointed two out of every three seasons. When a farmer's son wants a new bicycle, he tells the child to wait until the harvest is over to see whether the money's in the bank.

The Price of Perfection

So often parents encourage their children to reach perfection that the children expect perfection of themselves. I knew a young man who became so dependent on his high goals that he became overstressed—doctors eventually operated on him for a colostomy.

This fellow could open a chemistry book and literally memorize as he casually turned the pages. If his chemistry lab manual said that a normal student could complete a certain problem in fifteen minutes, this young man would look at the problem and think, "It takes ordinary mortals fifteen minutes to do this problem. I ought to finish it in ten minutes." Then if the problem took him fifteen minutes he became upset with himself.

The price of his perfection was not worth it. He may have tested twenty or thirty IQ points higher than his classmates, but his desire for perfection cost him his colon.

The bottom line in setting goals is to set them realistically within your potential or with your child's potential. If you try to run faster than you are able, you are setting yourself up for failure.

There is a saying, "It's better to shoot for the stars and land on the moon than shoot for the moon and land in the dirt."

This is a great saying for those who need to be pushed to reach their potential. However, for those who already push themselves a little too hard, this may set them up to fall short of the goal.

It is no small feat when reaching for the stars to remain happy should you land on the moon. Those who set their goals on Mount Everest need a strong handle on their emotional maturity to remain happy should they be forced to turn back.

17

Happiness
Mountains

Even when your children do not attain perfection, you can be happy with them and they can be happy with themselves. Refer to the drawing of a "Happiness Mountain." On this mountain are three hikers. Hiker A would like to reach 10,000 feet, but he only makes it to 8,000 feet. Hiker B would like to reach 7,000 feet, but he only reaches 6,000 feet. Hiker C would like to reach 3,000 feet, which he does.

As you consider these three hikers going up the mountain, which one is likely to be the most unhappy? Hiker A wanted to reach 10,000 feet, but he missed his goal by 2,000 feet. There is quite a great disparity between his goal and the point he reached. Hiker B wanted to reach 7,000 feet and only reached 6,000 feet. He missed his goal by 1,000 feet. Does that mean hiker C should be the most happy? Hiker C reached his goal. Yet, hiker A still stands the highest on the mountain and B still took second place.

Rather than seeing where they stand on the mountain, these hikers look at the disparity between their goals and

Failure Focus   Competitive Focus

10,000

8,000

7,000

6,000

3,000

Happiness Mountains

what they actually accomplished. The hiker with the greatest disparity between his goal and what he accomplished is often the most unhappy.

Failure Focus

Hiker A (the most unhappy because he missed his goal by the greatest distance) represents "failure focus." When the teacher puts a big "-7" instead of a " + 93" on your child's paper, she encourages failure focus. If your children despair when they don't reach the goals they seek, they succumb to failure focus. Too often hiker A, though far ahead of his peers, feels unhappy because he does not have everything.

Competitive Focus

On the other side of the mountain I have drawn three Boy Scouts. Boy Scout A reached 8,000 feet; Boy Scout B reached 7,000 feet; Boy Scout C reached 3,000 feet.

If you've ever seen Boy Scouts going up a mountain or getting in line for hot dogs, you know which Boy Scout is the happiest. The Scout who can get his second hot dog before anybody else has finished their first one feels the happiest. Likewise, the Boy Scout who is first when climbing a mountain feels the happiest.

Vince Lombardi was purported to have said, "Winning isn't everything; it's the only thing." The Boy Scouts demonstrate this attitude. I call the "winning is the only thing" attitude "competitive focus." Competitive focus will not lead to happiness any more than failure focus will.

Remember, half of the teams playing in ball games will lose. Does that mean everybody should quit playing ball? Five out of six racers in a one hundred – yard dash will not win. In a marathon hundreds of competitors will not finish first. Does that mean no one in the race can be happy except the winner? Does that mean ball games can't be enjoyed when half of those who play lose?

Notice that even though Boy Scout A and Hiker A reached the same place on the mountain, the Boy Scout is the happiest and the hiker is the most unhappy. The point is: it's not your altitude on the mountain that leads to happiness—it's your attitude.

With a failure focus you will always feel unhappy because you will never attain all your goals all the time. With a competitive focus, somebody will always break the record. Neither attitude leads to happiness for all participants.

Your child may not always reach the top of his class. He may not win the election for class president or be chosen as the captain of the ball team. He can still be happy if he learns how to enjoy the hike.

The hike may not always be easy. The hiker must learn to put one foot in front of the other. Sometimes he will take five steps forward and four steps back. Occasionally hikers run into a ravine—a parents' divorce or bankruptcy, death, illness, or any of the many tragedies of life.

Why do such pitfalls exist? To help us learn to hike. Climbing out of the pitfalls teaches people how to hike. Such pitfalls can make or break the hiker. If all life's hikes were in meadows, no one would ever grow or develop the ability to hike up mountains. Hikers learn how to enjoy the hike by maintaining the attitude: "I can be happy anywhere on the mountain because my happiness is not necessarily dependent upon my goals or where I am right now. Nor is it dependent on the others on the mountain. Happiness results from my decision to enjoy the hike."

Charity

Parents who learn to be happy with their children, regardless of how close the youngsters come to meeting their

145

parents' expectations, know something of charity. One way to practice charity, or the pure love of Christ, is to avoid negative feelings even when Junior falls short of the goals you desire for him.

The Apostle Paul talks about charity in 1 Corinthians 13. He is not writing here about putting money in the Salvation Army bucket. Paul said, "Though I bestow all my goods to feed the poor, and though I give my body to be burned [now that's a liquidation; you've not got much left to give], and have not charity, it profiteth me nothing." Obviously Paul did not mean "give" as most people think of giving. His definition of charity meant something other than, or in addition to, giving.

Paul includes in his definition of charity the traits of patience, long-suffering, enduring to the end. All these characteristics avoid negative feelings. Patience with a disobedient child, long-suffering when you must remind him again and again to behave, enduring to the end until he finally learns what you try to teach—this kind of charity means reducing anticipations and vulnerability to the failings of mortal men (or children).

Negative feelings can be avoided when you anticipate that things may indeed go wrong. Not everyone will reach the 10,000-foot mark on the mountain. This is a mortal world and everyone has mortal failings. Prepare yourself to deal appropriately with those failings.

Charity Toward Self

With whom do you find it most difficult to be charitable? You may find it difficult to be charitable towards the kids who run through the yard or the craftsmen who do not fix the sink the way you want or to your spouse who leaves towels on the bathroom floor. But the person you blame the most, who you wish could do more, and be better, is yourself. It is more difficult to be charitable towards yourself than towards anyone else.

Since people expect so much of themselves, as soon as they set a goal they immediately become emotionally dependent on its attainment. Then every little nuance of jeopardy between setting the goal and reaching it leaves them vulnerable to negative feelings.

So what do people do with all those negative feelings? They might either become depressed or take them out on somebody else. Faultfinding is the opposite of charity. Many times those who find fault with others have some negative feelings about themselves. To resist finding fault in others, it would help not to have the negative feelings about oneself. Charity towards others becomes much easier for those who develop charity towards themselves.

Recognize your human characteristics: you are mortal. Your goals can be eternal, yet you need to resist the tendency to become emotionally dependent on a goal. Then even if you don't reach the goal, you can still avoid negative feelings.

"Wait," you say. "We have been instructed to be like our Father in Heaven." In the New Testament, Matthew records Christ as saying: "Be ye therefore perfect, even as your Father which is in heaven is perfect" (Matthew 5:48). However, becoming perfect does not mean you have to be a "perfectionist."

I see many perfectionists in my office who are depressed and unhappy. They have set their hearts on goals which they have not reached. Setting your heart on a goal leaves you vulnerable to negative feelings. In addition, most of the time the goals are "of this world."

The Lord commanded us not to set our hearts on the things of this world: "Man should not counsel his fellow man, neither trust in the arm of flesh" (D&C 1:19). Murphy's law, "If anything can go wrong it will," implies in worldly terms a similar message. Because man can't count on anything but God, setting our hearts on the things of this world leaves us vulnerable to negative feelings.

Those who want to become truly perfect must reach the

goals God has set for man. A "perfectionist" seeks perfection in reaching his own goals, goals of this world and of his own making.

Paul summarized God's goals for man. He said that of faith, hope, and charity, the greatest is charity. One reason why could be that it is the hardest. And the hardest person to be charitable towards is yourself.

Children who learn to set their hearts on worldly goals also find it difficult to be charitable towards themselves. Seeking goals that are of this world is what leads to perfectionism. The hazards of raising a perfectionist child are evident. Overachievers are extremely vulnerable to negative feelings should they fail.

Hikers who learn failure focus and Boy Scouts who learn competitive focus are striving to succeed in the things of this world. You and your children can be happy wherever you are on the mountain when you seek God's rules for attaining perfection.

18

The Children
of Divorce

Ideally, children are reared in homes with two parents. However, the ideal is often not the case, and I am concerned about the many challenges facing single parents. All the principles in this book can benefit the single parent as much as traditional parents. But this final chapter is intended specifically as an aid to single parents and to those who are willing to be a resource to a single parent. Although sometimes fathers rear their children alone, I more often see single mothers facing this challenge. Therefore, this chapter is addressed to women who are rearing children alone.

Death used to be the significant event in an individual's childhood. However, polio, dyptheria, smallpox, strep, and staph infections now are subject to vaccinations and antibiotics. This has made death virtually a rare stranger to first- and second-generation young families. Only by automobile accidents and shocking events do the youthful precede the elderly in death.

Today divorce is the great trauma that death was in previous generations. When I began my child-psychiatry training, 90 percent of all children lived with both parents. Today 75 percent of all children do *not* live with both natural parents, and 26 percent of all children live with only one parent. The emotional damage divorce causes is tremendous, though not always obvious until sometimes even the grandchildren of divorce manifest symptoms.

Our divorce-riddled society does not encourage healthy negotiation and problem solving. Instead, society encourages problem solving through our legal system. The legal solution is an emotionally traumatic experience and is like a lottery with all parties clamoring to seize material goods. Legal solutions leave victors and victims but no real winners, except calloused attorneys on their way to the bank.

Dangers of Divorce

In a divorce where children are involved, the children are the losers. Not only are they deprived of two parents who are trusting, loving, cooperative, rewarding advocates who love one another but also are often presented with an embittered, guilty noncustodial parent and a reluctant stepparent.

In previous generations, the widow took Dad's picture off the mantle and said, "Son, here is a picture of your noble father. If he had any vices, I can't recall them. His beautiful memory includes many virtues for you to emulate (and a few more I'll slip in for good measure). Identify with him and you will be a fine young man."

Today I see too many divorcees pull the picture out from the bottom drawer. "Kid, here's a picture of your old man. If he had any virtues I don't remember them, but I can recite his faults. And you remind me of him—you're getting to be just like him!"

Both youngsters may have a spook held up as a male image but those images differ greatly.

While sons use their mother's expectations as role models, daughters strive to meet the father's expectations. In my experience, a divorce over a father's infidelity is absolutely devastating to a teenage daughter's trust. The vulnerability is that she will plunge into promiscuity, although an alert mother or therapist may thwart this tendency.

The family, the most basic child-rearing unit, is suffering a plague of divorce—like smallpox among the African natives. In addition, like diabetes, divorce runs in families. Once a pedigree suffers a single divorce, it affects the second, third, and fourth generations. The children of a divorce frequently have difficulty, without great effort and sometimes even with quality counseling, in negotiating a successful marriage, and few manage to experience a fiftieth anniversary.

Divorce is contagious: after one girl in an office gets a divorce, several others follow suit. My experience has led me to believe that most individuals who have experienced divorce wished they had seen a marriage counselor rather than a lawyer.

Divorce can threaten our civilization. For the last fifteen years, I have been counseling the grandchildren of divorced grandparents. The parents of these children struggle bravely; they are committed to their children, the family, and the marriage. But they didn't have an intimate, positive marital example, so they struggle to know how to be successful spouses and parents.

In interviewing divorced people ten and twenty years after a divorce I often discover much unresolved anger and grief, even when they are remarried. The normal dysfunction that accompanies a death lasts about one year. The funeral with it's formality and social support systems that accompany a death make it apparent to the bereaved that life will go on.

Divorce, on the other hand, is a dragged-out affair. For fifteen to twenty years wounds are reopened as children grow to maturity. There is no grave, no finality, no scars—only a festering wound.

No one can be entirely responsible for the good grace of another adult, particularly an ex-spouse. Yet professional therapy both before and after a divorce can do much to heal a wound. Such therapy can also help the divorcee develop a healthy relationship in a subsequent marriage.

The nuances between having and not having two natural parents are subtle: as Father stands in the park and tosses his youngster into the air, brushing the top of the child's head on the pine boughs, an anxious mother observes her little one flaying the air. She cries out, "Don't, you'll scare him." The natural father clutches the child to his comforting breast, teaching him to trust and to deal with anxiety, and says, "Don't worry, I'll be careful—he likes it."

However, too often the stepfather is told, "Leave him alone—he's *my* child." Stepfathers want to give their children the opportunity to experience anxiety, comfort, and then trust, just as a natural parent would. Children need a masculine input into their lives, the subtle benefits of which society is still documenting through research and studies.

It is easy enough in books on divorce to suggest that the parents can pretend, for the sake of the children, that they are still friends—as if the children cannot see through such a charade. Children wonder how their parents can separate and expect them to believe that they are still friends. Logically, friends could stay married, even if only for the child's sake.

Divorced parents are also instructed to tell their children, "It's not your fault," and "We'll always love you." How can a child trust his parents who once loved one another and now the noncustodial parent is remarried and more committed, both financially and timewise to the new family? The struggling single-parent family remains emotionally and financially deprived.

I am not satisfied to recommend a solution to divorce by suggesting there might be a method for dealing with the children of divorce. We must teach the parents of future generations to be emotionally healthy, thus helping them build successful marriages. Otherwise, divorce will be perpetuated and lead to future divorce.

Adultery, promiscuity, premarital sex, and teenage marriage have all undermined values conducive to marriage solidarity. Outlawing such vice will not end the divorce problem any more than prohibition ended alcoholism or raiding Bolivia will end the drug problems in the eighties.

I salute you who are working to raise emotionally healthy children. These children can become stable individuals and stable marriage partners.

The Single Parent's Needs

Single parents must make unusual effort to care for themselves. Many "good" parents are not prepared to look out for themselves nearly so well as they are prepared to care for others. They sacrifice and deny themselves, with all thought and energy directed to others. Such parents "burn out." It is essential that a single parent learn to care for their child's caretaker.

Sometimes I suggest the "Paper and Pencil Plan." Emotional resources need to be budgeted just like material resources. To budget emotional resources make a list:

1. Who can I emotionally afford to visit and help
   (a) once a year?
   (b) once a month?
   (c) once a week?
   (d) once a day?

2. Who is an unfailing resource in an emotional emergency?

3. Who is a 50/50 reciprocal friend?

4. Who must be carefully restrained and rationed lest they drain out every last bit of energy I need to survive?

5. Who are the cost-effective resources that bring more joy than sorrow, more resource than need?

Single parents, since they have no spouse to be a resource, are frequently bereft of positive emotions, so in addition to budgeting emotional resources they might need to "mine" them if they are not readily available. Self-help groups and church groups may help when it is clear that the ship will sink unless the present course is altered.

Single parents must also plan ahead for the material needs of themselves and their families. A higher dollar-per-hour income with less hours may become essential.

Plan ahead for emotional resources to help during child-rearing, particularly during adolescence. Supplemental parental adults (quasi-in-laws) are a great resource in child-rearing. These supplemental parents, like the apprentice's mentor, will need to invest in the children of a single parent throughout their childhood in order to be an appropriate resource later.

Very good adult friends may share their spouses in group child activities such as Little League and Scouting, or at events where teenagers need chaperones.

Just as birds need time off the roost, married couples need time off every eight to ten weeks—or oftener. Without guilt single parents need to arrange to leave their children well cared for while they attend an adult conference, visit a relative, or travel with friends.

Generous friends will want to take caution lest their help be misconstrued or misunderstood. A supplemental parent's friendshipping can easily become home-wrecking in both families.

Single parents need a chaperone even more than adolescents do, not because they are untrustworthy but because they want to maintain their good name and reputation. Lots of lights, early hours, and always a crowd of two or more adults will generally thwart suspicion.

The longest-lasting resources for the single parent come from within the family or through another marriage. A loving adult who is consistently available provides the most benevolent resource. Such a resource will provide an "emotional smorgasbord" which includes open, honest, gracious communication. Emotional nutrition is every bit as important as physical nutrition to the well-being of an individual.

The lessons you have learned in this book to help your children can also solve many problems that threaten an adult's happiness.

The principles of emotional nutrition can help those who have or will experience the divorce tragedy which is becoming so ubiquitous.

A total perspective on emotional health comes when you see how interrelated these chapters are. You may even find that you better understand earlier chapters in this book now that you have read the entire book.

19

Correct
Principles

Throughout the animal kingdom animals
are born at various stages of helplessness. Baby kittens, blind
for the first week of life, would perish without their mothers.
Ducks are born "ready to go." Ducklings can walk and swim
as soon as their feathers dry. They can even eat solid food.
Depending on the degree of independence each animal is
born with, the mother educates the baby until it no longer
needs her. Rabbits bear bunnies of their own after six
months; bears are nurtured by their mothers for two years.
Tigers spend day after day teaching their babies to stalk a
prey. Polar bears teach their young to fish and they protect
their young from enemies until their offspring are able to protect themselves. Though somewhat ironic, a good parent in
the animal kingdom is one who renders himself virtually un-
necessary.

People also raise their young so they can succeed on their
own. Whether human babies can survive without their own
nurturing parents is an idea that has intrigued many writers.

Authors have expressed the idea in fictional stories such as Rudyard Kipling's *The Jungle Book* and Edgar Rice Burrough's *Tarzan the Ape Man.*

Even if a child could survive physically without a parent, few doubt the necessity of educating a child's mind. Only after a decade or two of comprehensive instruction can a child succeed in a complex society, in which he needs to govern not only his behavior but also his emotions. As an adult he should be able to control himself without parental intervention. (This does not mean his parents cannot still be resources, just as the gospel, professional counselors, and higher education can be resources. But by this time he knows what is right and, if he desires, can choose to seek assistance in reaching his goals.)

Parents and experts both agree that parents must teach their children healthy behavior. Yet it is equally important that children learn to have healthy emotions. A broken arm received from falling out of a tree can heal. However, emotional scars that neither child nor parents know how to treat can be debilitating for life.

Many of the people I treat as adults are experts at governing their behavior, but emotionally they are infants. To live happy lives children need to control their own emotions. When someone else controls your emotions, someone else is in charge of your happiness.

One of the greatest things parents can teach their children to assure happiness is, "You are in charge of your mind." They can help their children develop thick skin.

I devoted the second half of this book specifically to governing emotions. You learned that children can avoid disappointment as they lower their anticipations, because everything will not happen as they would like. When they are not at the top of the mountain and when Santa doesn't leave everything in the Spiegel catalog, they can still be happy.

Often a child's emotions influence his behavior. In the first half of this book you learned to help your child govern his own behavior. The solutions offered there are based on the knowledge that a child's behavior is often influenced by his emotions.

A child learns to govern his behavior gradually: first in small areas and later, as he matures, in large areas. As children govern themselves well inside their pens, Mom and Dad enlarge their pens and give them more responsibility.

Although such an approach to child-reading seems simple, it takes a skilled parent to know when to hold a child's hand and when to stand back and let him walk on his own. The pages of this book have shared a number of ways to help parents determine the proper balance between being too strict and too permissive.

Often parents and children learn the hard way how much responsibility the child can handle. If at age two Junior slightly burns his finger in a candle, the consequence is not eternal and it will teach him to be wiser next time he is given the privilege of governing himself.

Childhood is practice for adult life. The more often you give a child the opportunity to govern himself rather than making decisions for him, the better prepared he will be to make *best* decisions when Mom and Dad are not around.

Sometimes it takes a few failures in business or politics before an adult achieves success. Likewise, you may have to allow your children to make some decisions on their own, even if they don't make the right decision, just to give them experience.

There comes a day when you cannot govern your children even if you want to. When your son has his own car, his own job, and his own apartment, you can't ground him, take away the car keys, or withhold his allowance. He must be able to govern himself wisely when he's twenty-one and tempted to rent X-rated movies or when he's forty-one and tempted to embezzle company funds.

The best way to assure that your son will make the correct decision at twenty-one and forty-one is to allow him some decision-making practice at age two and age ten. A fourteen-year-old who can be trusted at home alone for a weekend, who doesn't take the car, or throw wild parties, will be trustworthy at forty-one.

I have seen too many "adult-adolescent rebellions." Adults who have not been given the opportunity to make mistakes as youth often rebel when they are forty or fifty years old. They have been restrained by others their entire lives, rather than restraining themselves. Finally, when they are responsible for restraining themselves they choose not to do so.

Adults who experience adolescent rebellion may have extramarital affairs or indulge in gambling or try other taboos. Often such adults behaved well when they were children only because they feared the negative consequences. They never learned that doing what's right is a reward in itself. Like teenagers, they are intent on "bucking the system," whatever it may be.

I remember once when my seventeen-year-old daughter asked if she could go waterskiing on a Sunday. She wanted to go with a girlfriend and some of the interns at the hospital where she worked. I was concerned because I had known too many interns who would not have the best intentions when with a seventeen-year-old girl; besides, I wanted her to be in church on Sunday. I expressed my feelings and told her to make her own decision.

My daughter loved waterskiing more than any other sport. In addition, she was flattered by the attention of these very sought-after interns. But she told them no, she wouldn't go. Today she still marvels that at seventeen she made such a mature decision. She had had many years of practice in making decisions and had learned to make *best* decisions.

Although I frequently use my own experiences to illustrate a point, I recognize the danger in this. Just as you might expect a diet expert to have a slim body, you may expect a child-rearing "expert" to have perfect children. This isn't always so.

Were I to adopt a plan introduced long ago by our brother Lucifer, my children would indeed all be perfect. However, I have chosen not to govern my children in that way. I have chosen to teach them correct principles and let them govern themselves. Because they are free agents, sometimes they choose to follow my counsel and sometimes they don't.

Rearing children is one of the most difficult challenges in life. Whether your children choose to govern themselves as you would like or in another manner, you can find comfort if you have taught them what is right. In most situations, children who have been taught correct principles choose to abide by them. And you know that if they make *best* decisions while they are in your home, they will probably make *best* decisions throughout their lives.

Index